Which of you did it?

Problems of achieving criminal convictions when a child dies or is seriously injured by parents or carers

NSPCC

Cruelty to children must stop. FULL STOP.

Foreword and acknowledgements

For many years the National Society for the Prevention of Cruelty to Children (NSPCC) has been greatly concerned by cases where children die or are seriously injured at the hands of their parents or carers. Even though the evidence narrows the field of suspects down to a small group of potentially guilty parties, all too often no one is convicted of these dreadful crimes. This is clearly not achieving justice for children.

Each time another horrific tale hit the headlines, the NSPCC wrote to the relevant government departments to express our frustration with this area of the law, which we believe is failing children.

We have always been clear that we are not seeking unsafe convictions based on insufficient evidence. Rather we wish to find a way to get to the evidence that would be available if the defendants were to tell the truth.

The NSPCC has asked successive governments to, at the very least, research this vexing matter to try to understand it better, including considering how other jurisdictions address the problem. We received sympathetic responses, which shared our concerns, but none thought a dedicated research project the best way forward.

As our frustration grew, we organised a seminar titled "Which of you did it?" in July 2000. A panel of experts was invited to speak on the topic from a variety of perspectives:

> Police
> Health Services
> Social Services
> Academic
> Criminal Bar Association
> Crown Prosecution Service

This 'invitation only' event drew together individuals with a high level of expertise across a range of disciplines. Hearing the experts' presentations produced an air of excitement and optimism. It seemed that there was sufficient material pointing to potential solutions to merit further investigation of the issues. Subsequently the NSPCC invited these experts onto a working group to carry out these investigations.

The society was delighted that Her Honour Judge Isobel Plumstead agreed to chair the working group. The NSPCC is very grateful to the then Lord Chancellor's Department for agreeing to donate a great deal of her valuable time. Indeed, we are immensely grateful to every member of the working group, and to the organisations they represent, for their valuable time, their hard work and their devotion to tackling this very challenging problem. The working group met for just over a year and the results of its endeavours are in this report.

The death or serious injury of just one child at the hands of parents or carers is a tragedy, yet the problem is far greater than even the members of the working party had originally thought. There is a clear agenda. Both law and practice must be improved so that those who are responsible for these terrible crimes against innocent children can be brought to justice and children at risk can be properly protected.

Barbara Esam (Project Co-ordinator)
Lawyer, Public Policy Department
NSPCC

November 2003

About the working group

Her Honour Judge Isobel Plumstead, Chair

Isobel Plumstead has been a circuit judge since 2001. Called to the Bar in 1970, she practised as a barrister in London until 1990, when she was appointed to the principal registry of the family division as a district judge. She has been a crown court recorder and a member of the civil and family committees as well as the main board of the judicial studies board. Since the implementation of the Children Act 1989 in 1991 she has been nominated to try public and private law children cases at county court level. In 2002 she was authorised to sit as a deputy High Court judge in the family division and, in 2003, was made Designated Family Judge for Cambridge.

Detective Inspector Malcolm Bacon

Malcolm Bacon was a police officer for 30 years, retiring from Sussex Police at the end of November 2002. The majority of his service was with the CID. He served 10 years as a divisional detective inspector for Sussex, mainly in Brighton. In the latter years of his service, he was a member of Sussex's major crime branch, primarily involved in the investigation of homicide offences, either as the senior investigating officer or deputy. He has first hand knowledge of the problems involved in the prosecution of carers suspected of killing their children, having been the senior investigating officer in two high profile cases.

Barbara Esam
Project Co-ordinator

Barbara Esam is a lawyer in the public policy department of the NSPCC. Her post is focused on campaigning for improvements in legislation and policies that affect children in the civil and criminal jurisdictions. Previously Barbara was an assistant director of legal services in the law and administration department of an inner-London borough, where she was also the head of the social services legal section. She has worked in private practice specialising in family and child care law and youth justice.

Alison Kerr

Alison Kerr was admitted as a solicitor in 1973 and has been involved in prosecuting since 1975. She was employed in Derbyshire and Nottinghamshire before being appointed as Chief Crown Prosecutor for Lincolnshire in 1999. She is a member of the Crown Prosecution Service (CPS) board. Alison has always taken an interest in cases involving abuse of children. She has worked co-operatively with other agencies to improve procedures in these cases and was a national tutor for the CPS. Alison is a lead tutor for "Speaking up for Justice", the legislative provisions to assist vulnerable and intimidated witnesses in giving their evidence.

Christopher Kinch QC

Christopher Kinch practises from chambers at 23 Essex Street in London and is a member of the Criminal Bar Association. He took Silk in 1999 and prosecutes and defends in a range of serious cases. He also sits in the Crown Court as a Recorder.

Dr Jean Price MB, BS, D.Obs, RCOG, DPH, DPM, FRCPCH

Jean Price is a consultant paediatrician for Southampton City Primary Care Trust where she leads a team of doctors examining all child abuse cases within the trust, and the more complicated ones from across the region. She is a member of both the Southampton and South West Hampshire Area Child Protection Committees (ACPCs).

Jean has worked with children since 1974 and more specifically in the field of child abuse since 1983. Jean was a police surgeon for Avon & Somerset Constabulary for 15 years, while working as a consultant paediatrician in Bristol. She was a member of the Department of Health (DH) and Royal College of Paediatrics working party on fictitious and induced illness.

Detective Superintendent Steve Scott

Detective Superintendent Steve Scott joined Sussex's Police Force in 1977 and transferred to Surrey as Head of Intelligence in September 2002. He has worked in a variety of roles, but predominantly in the CID and serious crime. He is responsible for sensitive policing issues including covert policing, surveillance teams and the Force Intelligence Unit. Since 1997 Steve has been a Senior Investigating Officer leading murder investigations. Whilst in Sussex as Head of Specialist Investigations Branch he took responsibility for violent crime policies including child protection, domestic violence and hate crime.

Professor John R Spencer QC

John Spencer is a professor of law at the University of Cambridge and a fellow of Selwyn College, where he was an undergraduate in the 1960s. He specialises in the law of criminal evidence and procedure and has written widely on this subject.

Andrew Webb

Andrew Webb is Director of Social Services for Cheshire. He was previously county manager of Cheshire children's services and assistant director (children) with Knowsley Metropolitan Borough Council. Andrew has worked in local authority social services, primarily with children and families, since 1976. He is currently chair of the Cheshire Area Child Protection Committee (ACPC) and is one of the Association of Directors of Social Services leads on child protection matters. He was a member of the DH steering groups overseeing the development of: Working Together; the Framework for the Assessment of Children in Need; the national plan to protect children from commercial sexual exploitation; and joint guidance on fabricated and induced illness in children.

Contents

A. Summary of recommendations

It became clear early on that the working group's recommendations would focus mainly on early co-operation and co-ordination. Accordingly much that the group recommends is addressed to the various professionals concerned with frontline child protection and the government departments responsible for them.

The area of law reform is more difficult. More research is needed to provide reliable figures on the incidence of serious offences against children. Some of the law reforms discussed in this report would inevitably impinge on the human rights of others. Justification of law reform must be on the basis that it is a proportionate response to the need.

The working group calls on the Department for Constitutional Affairs, the Home Office, the Department for Education and Skills (DfES) and the Department of Health (DH) to co-ordinate their responses to its recommendations:

1. **Undertake research to establish the true incidence of serious assaults upon young children.**

2. **Undertake a thematic review of police and prosecution processes to establish best practice principles.**

3. **Establish inter-disciplinary protocols at a national level for the investigation of injuries that may be the result of criminal assaults.**

4. **Issue a consultation paper to the relevant professional groups to consider the feasibility and benefits of mandatory reporting.**

5. **Clarify the law in relation to the admissibility at trial of evidence of previous acts of violence.**

6. **Consider enhancing the powers of judges in criminal cases to ensure that the experts are appropriately qualified and experienced, whether the evidence is to be adduced by the prosecution or the defence.**

7. **Draft new legislation to require those who had responsibility for the care of a child who suffered injury to account for the period when the injury was sustained. Adverse inferences could be drawn where the carer fails to give an account.**

8. **Consider the potential for new legislation to provide that where someone has a duty of care towards a child they may have injured, there will be a case to answer.**

9. The Sentencing Advisory Panel should review sentencing for offences of violence against children.

10. Consider the development of a national register of offenders who have committed offences of violence against children.

B. Report of the working group

Introduction

Each week three infants suffer serious injury or death when in the care of adults who should be protecting them. The statistics show that less than a third of cases reported to the police result in an adult actually being prosecuted to conviction. In most of these cases, the persons who had care of the child at the time the child suffered injury are readily identified, yet prosecutions regularly fail or are not even undertaken. Far too often the reason is the lack of evidence to prove which of two, or a small number of suspects, actually caused the injury or death.

The NSPCC's "Which Of You Did It?" working group began meeting in 2001 and drew together professionals and academics from a range of disciplines. The objective of the NSPCC in setting up the group was to identify whether changes should be called for in the law or procedures concerning the investigation of death or serious injury to children. The NSPCC hoped that the work of the group would further draw attention to the problem, which was highlighted at the Society's July 2000 seminar on the subject in London.

The working group sought to gather evidence and statistics from the medical, social services, police, academic and legal professions. Its deliberations continued into 2002 and the individual and collective views of its members were presented at a well-attended consultative conference at the University of Cambridge in November 2002 which was followed by a further period of consultation. The timing has turned out to be propitious. The Law Commission (which had representatives attending the working group as observers) has taken up the challenge and its proposals[1] on this subject are now well advanced. There is reason to believe that there is support for reform within the Government.

While the debate has moved on since the working group presented its proposals to the Cambridge conference, its members trust there will be value in putting forward a summary of the group's final reflections. The proposals fall into three categories:

1. Improvements in investigations
2. Improving trial procedures
3. Substantive law reform.

1. Improvements in investigations

1.1 Incidence

The figures for "reported crimes" are likely to underestimate the incidence of serious assaults upon young children. Many assaults do not come to the attention of health professionals and

---

[1] Children: Their non-accidental death or serious injury (Criminal Trials): a consultative report. *The Law Commission (Law Com. No 279) April 2003.*

social workers, and then to the police until a child suffers a later injury, possibly fatal. Evidence of earlier injury then emerges when a full skeletal x-ray is performed, or witnesses describe having seen marks upon the child.

Injuries seen by professionals, such as family doctors, nursery or hospital staff should be reported to social services under *Working Together*[2] procedures, but may not be reported to police.

> **Recommendation 1:**
> Research should be undertaken to establish the true incidence of serious assaults upon young children.

1.2 Thematic Review

There should be a thematic review of the police and prosecution processes, examining their practice at every stage from initial reporting to the trial. The conclusions of a thorough review, together with lessons learned from reviews under Chapter 8 of Working Together and of other similar inquiries, should be used in formulating the requirements for working protocols.

> **Recommendation 2:**
> There should be a thematic review of police and prosecution processes to establish best practice principles.

1.3 Investigation protocols

In a high proportion of cases investigated by the police the investigating team decides that there is insufficient evidence to justify charges, or the Crown Prosecution Service (CPS) discontinues the prosecution on the grounds that the evidence is not sufficient to afford a reasonable prospect of conviction. Where two carers may have been suspects the available evidence often does not go far enough to establish that one rather than the other inflicted the injury, or that both were responsible in the sense that it can be proved that they acted in concert, the doctrine of "joint enterprise".

Much can and should be done to facilitate and improve the investigative processes at this early stage. Delay in commencing investigations is always undesirable. Police need to go to accredited experts straight away when an investigation starts, even before a suspect is known. A national lead should be taken to establish interdisciplinary protocols for the investigation of injuries that may be the result of criminal assaults. Items that may be of significance, for example, clothing and bedding, should be preserved. The responses and presence of significant persons should be recorded with care. Templates for standard communication and information sharing with other agencies should be established. Inter-disciplinary investigations should be the norm from the start of the investigation, encompassing the knowledge and experience from all groups, including paediatricians, pathologists and radiologists.

A paediatric pathologist with forensic experience should either carry out any post-mortem examination, or it should be carried out jointly by a forensic and a paediatric pathologist.

---

[2]*Department of Health (DH); Home Office; Department for Education and Employment (DfEE) (1999):* Working together to safeguard children: a guide to inter-agency working to safeguard and promote the welfare of children. *London: The Stationery Office.*

Recommendation 3:
Inter-disciplinary protocols for the investigation of injuries that may be the
result of criminal assaults should be established at a national level.

1.4 Reporting

Early reporting by the hospital to the police of serious and fatal injuries suspected to have been
non-accidental should be a key component of all protocols. Consideration should be given to
making the requirement mandatory. The working group found that among the wide range of
professionals who attended the Cambridge conference there was strong support for mandatory
reporting to police of suspicious deaths and injuries to children. The statutory provisions which
permit investigators to seek access to medical and other confidential records, including previous
injuries/admissions should be used more and earlier in appropriate cases. Consideration should
be given to permitting access to the records of siblings as well.

The objective should be to gather information systematically and effectively, from the earliest
involvement of the emergency services, without impeding medical treatment or protective
measures. If this is achieved, a significantly greater number of cases will cross the evidential
threshold and enable proceedings to be taken.

Recommendation 4:
A consultation paper should be issued to the relevant professional groups to
consider the feasibility and benefits of mandatory reporting.

2. Improving trial procedures

2.1 Previous violence

The working group was concerned that evidence of earlier violence by a suspect towards a
child may be available, yet not adduced in evidence. Where there is evidence of previous
violence towards the child, prosecutors sometimes appear reluctant to rely on such evidence
notwithstanding its probative value, and when they seek to do so judges may exclude such
evidence upon the basis that its probative value is outweighed by the prejudicial effect.

If there is evidence of previous violence towards other children, there may be sufficient
similarities, "striking similarity", to render such evidence admissible. Again the group was
concerned that prosecutors may be reluctant to seek to rely on such evidence, and judges
reluctant to admit it, when to do so may result in an appeal.

In short the law is in need of clarification. The Court of Appeal should have the opportunity to
consider, in if possible more than one appeal, guidelines for first instance judges trying cases of
this nature. The right of the Crown to appeal preliminary binding rulings has as yet been little
used. The working group would encourage prosecutors to seek rulings in order that the criteria
can be considered authoritatively.

Recommendation 5:
The law needs clarification in relation to the admissibility at trial of
evidence of previous acts of violence.

2.2 Expert evidence

The working group was concerned that in some criminal trials there is a risk that judges, magistrates, or juries may be misled, or the effect of scientific evidence distorted, where "experts" of doubtful reputation, inappropriate experience or expertise, or lacking in impartiality, can be relied upon in court, provided that the very basic rules for the service of expert evidence have been complied with.

The use of expert evidence in civil and family proceedings is now subject to considerable court control. Not only is early disclosure in advance of proceedings where pre-action protocols apply provided for, the court can and does control the use of expert evidence to ensure that the evidence admitted is relevant and the expert appropriately qualified and experienced. An agreement of admissible expert evidence between defence and prosecution at a pre-trial hearing should be encouraged.

> **Recommendation 6:**
> Consideration should be given to enhancing the powers of judges in criminal cases to ensure that the experts called are appropriately qualified and experienced, whether the evidence is to be adduced by the prosecution or the defence.

3. Substantive law reform

The issue of reform of the substantive law in this area was the most difficult the working group had to deal with. While current law is failing to meet the challenge of the problem, reform must not take the form of a "quick fix" that leads only to unfairness and confusion. The group was greatly encouraged and assisted by the interest shown in its work by the Law Commission, and in particular by His Honour Judge Alan Wilkie QC and Phil Bates. The working group wishes them every success in the task of taking this issue forward, and how they will give particular attention to Recommendations 7 and 8 (see below).

3.1 Inferences from silence

The group's starting point was that there is a compelling moral case that a carer who assumes responsibility for a child has a duty to account for any serious injury that has happened to the child to the best of his or her ability. The working group can see no reason why that duty should not be enshrined in statute. However, it is not desirable that an offence of failing or refusing to answer questions when called upon to do so by investigators should be created.

All this is not to concede that a failure to give an explanation for a child's injuries should be without consequences. A suspect in any criminal investigation is not obliged to answer the questions of investigators, although a jury may, in certain circumstances, be invited to draw adverse inferences, but only to support other evidence sufficient to constitute a prima facie case, if he does.

There is a need for the enactment of provisions similar to those in Sections 34 and 36 of the Criminal Justice and Public Order 1994, so as to provide that, when it is established that a person, whether alone or with others, had responsibility for the care of a child who suffers injury, he or she is under an obligation to account for the period during which the injury was suffered.

An unjustified failure to explain would lead to the risk of an adverse inference being drawn.

> **Recommendation 7:**
> New legislation should be drafted to require those who had responsibility
> for the care of a child who suffers injury to account for the period when
> the injury was sustained. Adverse inferences could be drawn where the
> carer fails to give an account.

3.2 Lane and Lane[3]

Members of the working group were unanimous in the view that "across the board" reversal of the decision would be unsatisfactory and may lead to serious injustice in cases where the special circumstance of the existence of responsibility for a vulnerable dependent child, do not exist.

The group would welcome, albeit with caution, consideration of whether legislation should be introduced to provide that where each of two people who may have injured a young child has a duty of care towards that child, their opportunity to have committed the assault would give rise to "a case to answer". This would place each carer in the position of having to choose whether to present evidence in his or her defence instead, as at present, requiring the court to withdraw the case from the jury.

There will inevitably still be cases where, no evidence having been called by the defence, the judge will have to rule on whether there is a case to go to the jury. The group knows the Law Commission is keenly aware of the risk that a conviction would be vulnerable if it was deemed to have been obtained mainly on an inference from the defendants' silence and echoes its acknowledgement of the need to:

> "Provide a reasonable balance between the State's obligations to the child
> under the UN Convention and the ECHR [European Convention on
> Human Rights] and its obligations to a defendant under Article 6 of the
> ECHR."[4]

The group rejected, as being incompatible with the right to a fair trial under Article 6, the possibility of requiring carers to answer questions in a criminal investigation and making their answers admissible against themselves and others.

> **Recommendation 8:**
> Consideration should be given to the potential for new legislation, which
> would provide that where someone has a duty of care towards a child they
> may have injured, there will be a case to answer.

---

[3] *Lane and Lane (1987) 82 CrAppR 5; child of 22 months, killed by the effects of a single blow; parents convicted at trial of manslaughter; manslaughter conviction quashed because of uncertainty as to which one was present when the blow was struck; qualifying the earlier case-law (particularly Gibson and Gibson (1985) 80 CrAppR 24) the Court of Appeal held that, in such a situation, the prosecution has failed even to establish a case to answer; cruelty convictions under s.1 CYPA 1933 were upheld for related injuries in respect of which there was other evidence.*
[4] Children: Their non-accidental death or serious injury (Criminal Trials): a consultative report. *The Law Commission (Law Com. No 279) April 2003.*

3.3 Sentencing

Parliament has reflected the revulsion of society at cruelty to and neglect of children by increasing the maximum sentence for the offence to 10 years and the "tariff" has increased accordingly. It is clear also that the Court of Appeal has upheld substantial sentences in cases of manslaughter, and wounding or inflicting grievous bodily harm "with intent", where the maximum sentence is life imprisonment.

Without specific intent to cause serious harm having been proved or admitted, the maximum sentence of five years for causing serious injury to a vulnerable and defenceless child is, in the view of the working group, too short. There is some concern that the maximum sentence of 10 years imprisonment for offences of wilful neglect or cruelty does not leave enough "headroom" at the top for the worst cases. The Sentencing Advisory Panel should be asked to consider offences of violence against children.

The rehabilitative and protective purposes of sentencing may be furthered by extension of the powers of the courts to impose periods of post-release supervision and extended periods of licence.

> **Recommendation 9:**
> The Sentencing Advisory Panel should review sentencing for offences of violence against children.

3.4 Offenders' register

The Sex Offenders' Register is believed to be an effective means of monitoring the movements and associations of those listed but it is confined to registration of those convicted of certain specific offences. Information about those with a history of ill-treating children is not just confined to criminal records. In family proceedings, particularly care proceedings, there are on occasions specific findings (to the civil standard) that a named person has been violent towards a child or children. Some government departments have a duty to maintain records of those believed to be unsuitable to have unsupervised contact with children. Local authority social services departments may have information in child protection files and in consequence of children being on the child protection register.

It has proved difficult to provide a system of police checks for those working with children and there are serious concerns about the accuracy of criminal records. Consideration should be given to the national registration of relevant and reliable information, from civil as well as criminal proceedings. The working group was unanimous in the view that criminal convictions for these offences should be on a register. Access to and the dissemination of such information should be carefully controlled. The aim is to further the protection of children, for while bringing an offender to justice must be the desire of a civilised society, the working group's members have no wish to encourage public disorder.

> **Recommendation 10:**
> Consideration should be given to the development of a national register of offenders who have committed offences of violence against children.

C. Contributions from working group members

The following contributions from members of the working group are expanded versions of the papers presented at the NSPCC's conference held at the University of Cambridge in November 2002. At the conference each member considered how his or her particular discipline could help to bring more successful proceedings against those who harm children.

i) The police perspective

Detective Superintendent Steve Scott and Detective Inspector Malcolm Bacon, Sussex Police

1. Introduction

The background to this issue for Sussex Police involved the sudden death of an eight-week-old boy in Brighton in March 1997. As there were concerns regarding the family generally in relation to neglect issues a Home Office approved pathologist carried out a post-mortem on the child. The results were inconclusive, and the cause of death put down as sudden infant death syndrome (SIDS).

The child protection team (CPT) was still concerned and continued its enquiries into the family. It was quickly established that the carers, a 24-year-old woman and her common-law husband of 36, had also been the carers of two other children who had died while in their care. One of these children was their own seven-month-old son, the other a six-week-old nephew. On each occasion the cause of death had been recorded as natural, although there were traumatic events leading up to both.

The police began an investigation. The large amount of evidence gathered pointed to suffocation as a common cause of these deaths. In the case of each child two minutes would have been enough to achieve the necessary physiological effect leading to death. Further investigation concluded that in every case only the two carers had the necessary time to carry out the assault. They were both arrested on suspicion of being responsible for the murders of the three children. In interview the man declined to answer questions, responding with "no comment" throughout. The woman did provide an account, which described continual domestic abuse. She concluded her statement by alleging her partner had suffocated all three. Both were charged with murder, under joint enterprise, and were sent for trial.

The case was heard at Lewes Crown Court. Once the prosecution case had been heard the defence submitted an argument of "no case to answer". This argument was heard over a number of days, leading eventually to the trial adjudicating that the prosecution had been unable to differentiate which of the defendants, either individually or together, had carried out the assault leading to the deaths. The murder charge was dismissed.

The two later appeared at the same court on charges of cruelty and neglect, leading to terms of imprisonment of two years and two and a half years for the woman.

The trial and its outcome caused a huge outcry in Sussex generally and Brighton in particular. The local county newspaper campaigned on the issue, saying that it was morally and legally wrong to know that one or other had committed murder but that neither could be successfully prosecuted. Petitions collected signatures locally and there was a call for a public enquiry. Detective Inspector Malcolm Bacon, the senior investigating officer in the case, met Jack Straw MP, then Home Secretary, in April 2000 to discuss the issues. In a letter Mr Straw said the Home Office at that stage was seriously considering the matter and suggested that an offence of "causing the death of a person through neglect/cruelty" could be introduced. This would attract a higher sentence, with a maximum of 14 years imprisonment.

2. The police's role within the working group

To establish the scale of the problem by looking at the frequency of cases similar to that outlined above, members of the working group were asked to examine key areas within their disciplines. The police task was to carry out a scoping exercise to establish the extent of "Which of You Did It?" incidents in England and Wales.

In order to achieve this, Terence Grange, the Chief Constable of Dyfed-Powys and Association of Chief Police Officers' (ACPO) crime committee lead on child protection wrote to all forces requesting the following information:

- The number of children suspected of being killed unlawfully or receiving serious injury (GBH) between 1 January 1998 and 31 December 2000, where there were more than one parent/carer who could possibly have been responsible for the injuries. The victims were divided into four age ranges – up to six months, six months to two years, two to five years and five to 10 years

- The number of these cases which were not proceeded with following advice from Crown Prosecution Service

- The number of cases dismissed at Court

- The number that resulted in acquittal

- The number successfully prosecuted

- The youngest age at which a child has given evidence in connection with these types of proceedings

- Any additional information regarding:
  - good practice in successful case prosecution
  - adverse rulings which have frustrated the prosecution.

The police representative also undertook to review the Office for National Statistics' (ONS) published mortality rates regarding homicide and probable homicide in England and Wales.

3. Legal problems with injuries inflicted by one or other parent/carer – the extent of incidents in England and Wales

3.1 Aim

The aim of this section is to use data supplied by individual police forces in England and Wales to enable a more detailed understanding of the cases of death or serious injury to young children. It focuses on analysis of data gathered by Sussex Police on behalf of the ACPO crime committee relating to

1. The age profile of such victims.
2. The extent to which successful prosecutions were brought.

This section puts these findings into the context of a study by the ONS into trends in homicide and, using both sets of material, draws conclusions as to:

• Whether young children are disproportionately victims of such offences

• How likely such cases are to result in a successful prosecution.

3.2 Background

The Sussex Police's crime management department collated responses to the letter sent in April 2001 by Terence Grange, Chief Constable of Dyfed-Powys Police. Responses were received from 40 of the 43 forces to which the request was sent. These 40 forces identified 492 children aged 10 years and under who had been unlawfully killed or who had received a serious injury between 1 January 1998 and 31 December 2000. Forces were asked to divide the ages of victims into four categories (see table 1).

Forces were additionally asked for details of how many cases had reached a successful conclusion and, where this had not been the case, the reasons why.

3.3 Victims

Of the 492 children identified, details of age groups were supplied for 476 victims (the discrepancy was caused by two forces supplying a total figure for the number of victims aged under 10 years, but who gave no details as to how these were broken down into the categories requested).

Table 1: Numbers by age group categories of children unlawfully killed or who had received a serious injury between 1 January 1998 and 31 December 2000.

Age category	Number of victims
0 to 6 months	239
6 months to 2 years	155
2 years to 5 years	48
5 years to 10 years	34
Total	**476**

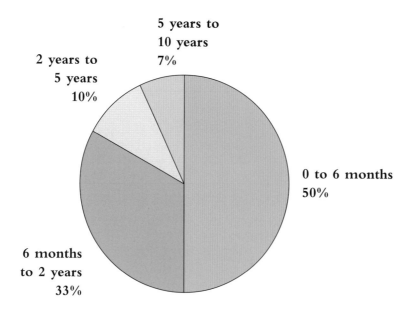

(Source: Sussex Police Force Crime Management Department)

Figure 1: Proportion by age group categories of children unlawfully killed or who had received a serious injury between 1 January 1998 and 31 December 2000.

It can be seen that, within this sample, the risk of being a victim of death or serious injury decreases very significantly with age. The combined two lowest age groups, from birth to two years, or one fifth of the age range encompassed by the sample, account for 83 per cent of victims.

These findings, based on data supplied by police forces, appear consistent with national figures for homicide rates in England and Wales, published by the ONS in an article in a 1999 issue of *Health Statistics Quarterly* entitled 'Recent trends in deaths from homicide in England and Wales'. (NB. the ONS figures encompass homicide and "probable homicide" only, and do not incorporate serious injury as with the figures supplied to Sussex Police.)

Using registration information supplied by coroners in England and Wales for the five year period 1993 to 1997, this study found that:

- By far the highest homicide rates for both males and females was amongst infants aged under one year, where there were 44 homicides per million per annum in males and 35 per million in females

- Once past infancy, rates fell rapidly to the point where they were lowest in both sexes between the ages of five and 14 years

- Rates rose again in young adults, particularly for men, peaking at 33 per million in their early 20s before falling steadily until the age of 80

- Homicides amongst adult women exhibited a similar pattern, though peaking at 15 per million at age 24

- Death rates due to homicide are invariably higher in males than in females with the gap being highest amongst young adults and lowest in children aged under 10 and adults aged over 80. (Source: ONS)

Figure 2: Average age-specific mortality rates from homicide and probable homicide in England and Wales between 1993 and 1997, by sex.

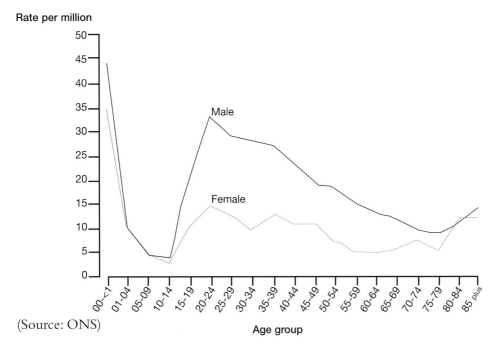

(Source: ONS)

Figure 3 below provides more detail on the male to female homicide rate for infants aged less than one year and shows how this has altered over an extended period between 1979 and 1997. The graph shows that, as with the population as a whole (see above), male infants are invariably more likely than females to be a victim of homicide:

Figure 3: Infant homicide rates in England and Wales between 1979 and 1997, by sex.

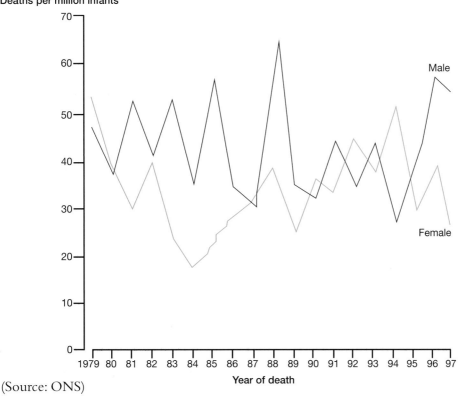

(Source: ONS)

The ONS research also included statistics on the causes of death registered by coroners in England and Wales for the five year period 1993 to 1997. The study found that amongst infant killings, where victims were less than one year old:

- Over 60 per cent were due to skull fracture or intra-cranial injury, including haemorrhage

- About 10 per cent were from suffocation or strangulation

- About 20 per cent were due to either other or unspecified kinds of injury.

This was contrasted with a very different pattern of injury at other ages. In older children there were very few head injuries whilst asphyxia, poisoning, and other, unspecified causes accounted for more than 60 per cent of homicides. (Source: ONS)

3.4 Reasons for not bringing a successful prosecution

Of the 492 victims identified by the request to police forces from Chief Constable Grange, details were received of 366 cases which had either been brought to a conclusion in court, or which had been discontinued prior to court. Given that the letter was written on 4 April 2001, it is likely that much of the discrepancy between the two figures is accounted for by cases still under investigation.

Table 2: Outcomes of cases of children unlawfully killed or who had received a serious injury between 1 January 1998 and 31 December 2000.

Outcome	Number of cases
Successful	99
Acquitted	21
Dismissed	21
No further action★	225
Total	**366**

(★Includes both police and Crown Prosecution Service)
(Source: Sussex Police Force Crime Management Department)

Figure 4: Proportion by outcome of cases of children unlawfully killed or who had received a serious injury between 1 January 1998 and 31 December 2000.

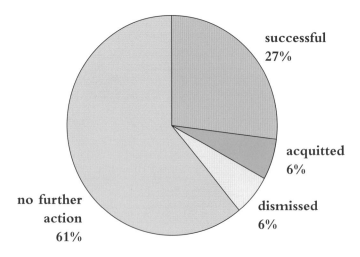

successful
27%

acquitted
6%

dismissed
6%

no further
action
61%

(Source: Sussex Police Force Crime Management Department)

It can be seen that a successful prosecution was brought in a little over one quarter of cases and that this was largely due to the fact that the majority did not reach court at all.

Given that the average number of cases supplied was nine per force, extreme caution should be exercised when making comparisons between outcomes of cases in individual forces. Nonetheless a wide discrepancy exists amongst the forces which reported the two largest number of cases. The figures supplied by West Midlands show that this force reached a successful prosecution in 50 per cent of cases (16 out of 32), which represents almost twice the rate for police forces as a whole. Essex, by contrast, reported 48 cases with just four successful prosecutions, or eight per cent, with the remaining 44 all categorised as "no further action". It could be, therefore, that examples of good practice exist in some forces that warrant further investigation. Forces were also asked the youngest age at which a child has given evidence in connection with such proceedings. While 11 did so, the majority reported either "no data" or "no children gave evidence". These 11 were spread evenly within the range five to eight years.

3.5 Research conclusions

Information supplied by 40 police forces in England and Wales on 392 child victims of death or serious injury during a three year period has provided evidence that infants aged under two years make up a hugely disproportionate number (83%) of child victims under 10 years old.

These findings appears to complement research previously published by the ONS which showed that infants aged under one year were by far the most likely of all age groups to be victims of homicide - approximately 10 times more likely than the five to 14 age group.

The second part of the Sussex Police study found that perpetrators of child murder, manslaughter, and serious injury are unlikely to be successfully prosecuted. Only a quarter of cases for the period for which data was requested was successfully prosecuted.

4 Summary of issues for further discussion

The debate within the working group has highlighted a number of questions for further consideration:

- Should an offence of causing death of a child through neglect or cruelty attract a higher sentence than the current ten year maximum?

- Could the Sussex Joint Agency Protocol: Unexplained Child Deaths be adopted nationally? This protocol gives an inter-agency investigation a template for response, information sharing, preservation of evidence and guidelines for agency liaison (See Appendix)

- Should a framework for inter-agency training regarding unexplained child deaths and working to a joint agency protocol be created for use nationally? (See page 25 for a thematic review)

- Should medical records, both of the victim and siblings, be available without knowledge or consent of the parents/carers/suspects?

- Should previous convictions and previous investigations for similar offences be made known in court?

- Should the degree of admissibility of similar fact evidence change?

- Should the status of Lane and Lane change?

- Should the "right to silence" and failure to give an explanation where it would be reasonable to do so be re-appraised?

- Can the courts improve the quality control of expert evidence, its weighting, value and inclusion?

- How can the record keeping within A&E of words used and reasons given on first attendance by parent/carers be improved?

- How can generic issues arising from Part 8 Reviews nation-wide be properly addressed?

- Should there be a national register of offenders? (See below for the case for a national register).

A case for a thematic review in relation to the investigation and prosecution of offenders responsible for the death or serious injury of a child

Detective Inspector Malcolm Bacon, Sussex Police

1. Background

1.1 The investigation of a child death or serious injury, particularly where there is a suspicion that the child may have been unlawfully assaulted, must be considered as one of the most significant events coming to the attention of authorities. It must be investigated thoroughly and prosecuted successfully whenever possible, and use the most experienced and professional staff available from all the relevant agencies.

1.2 The Home Secretary, David Blunkett, speaking in December 2001 said: "Protecting children is the highest priority for this government and I will continue to work hard towards making our society as safe as possible for them."

1.3 Despite this commitment, figures recently compiled show that only 27 per cent of cases involving the homicide or serious injury of a child in England and Wales, where it was suspected that either one or the other of the carers were involved, actually resulted in successful prosecution.

1.4 Notwithstanding the current problems in relation to the prosecution of offenders covered by the joint enterprise or "cut throat" defences, it must be accepted that there are a number of problems with regard to the efficient and effective gathering of potential evidence. This should start prior to the event and before the initial call and attendance, continuing through the medical procedures, police involvement and be ongoing with all the other relevant agencies.

1.5 In a number of cases some of the issues may have been investigated within the Part 8 Review process. But what Part 8 is not intended to address is the potential of effective and efficient evidence gathering to support a successful prosecution of the offender.

2. Methodology

The research outlined above highlights that some police forces manage a high detection and prosecution rate, whilst others seem to be less successful.

2.1 With this in mind, an in-depth scrutiny of the relevant cases should be fully explored to examine and ascertain where potential evidence has been identified and collated, and where further potential opportunities could be available to the investigation. It would also identify why some areas of the country are more successful in obtaining convictions.

2.2 This scrutiny should incorporate all available information prior to the crime, including:

- Prior police involvement
- Social services involvement
- Previous medical evidence
- Domestic history

- School records
- NSPCC involvement
- Any other support groups, etc.

2.3   At the time of the event coming to the attention of the various agencies, what potential evidence was available, including:

- 999 calls
- Paramedic/ambulance staff
- Medical admissions
- Paediatric examination
- Police procedures
- Forensic use and availability
- Liaison with HM Coroner
- Post-mortem procedures
- Expert evidence
- CPS advice and involvement.

2.4   Questions to be asked at this point include:

- What evidence gathering procedures and processes are being used?
- Is there consistency in the processes?

2.5   Prior to any research being undertaken, consultation should take place with all of the relevant agencies to ascertain what they would require from such a review, or indeed what they would wish to see included.

2.6   There should be general availability of the various records, and anonymity guaranteed to the identified parties. It is the principles and obstructions to successful prosecutions that are being examined and explored, not any individual actions or enquiry.

2.7   Once the data has been collated, it could then be shared with other professionals from within each agency for explanation where necessary, validation, clarification, rationale, accuracy of fact and emphasis and most importantly for good working practices, which can be shared further.

3. Problems considered

3.1   To be successful, the review team would have to be mindful of the following:

- Credibility of the review team and the processes involved
- Trust and support from the various agencies in the process
- Availability of the data
- Interpretation of the data
- Local/national guidelines which impact on the evidence gathering process
- Honesty and openness
- Staffing for the review process
- Resources available
- Funding
- Administrative support.

4. Resulting practices

4.1 When the evidence has been collated and analysed it would be possible to publish a manual, highlighting good working practices from all agencies and consideration of a working protocol. (Building on the Joint Agency Protocol published by Sussex Police and partners – see Appendix)

4.2 A consistent national training package could be created, which would allow all agencies, either individually or as part of joint training initiatives, to improve their performance. The manual could then be considered as a dynamic working document for all the agencies involved in these tragedies.

The case for a national register of offenders in relation to child abuse

Detective Inspector Malcolm Bacon, Sussex Police

For some years now there has been a national register of sex offenders. The investigating agencies consider this an excellent tool to keep tabs on these potential offenders. It has been accepted that on occasions it can be an extremely labour intensive task to keep the register up-to-date, but overall the pros well and truly out balance the cons.

I am suggesting that there ought to be a similar national register in relation to offenders, either convicted of offences under Section 1 of the Children Act 1989, or where a judgement of a potential offence has been made by a judge in family proceedings.

The reasons are hopefully self-explanatory: often there are occasions where an itinerant known offender can move into a potentially weak family situation and abuse children, either physically or emotionally, without ever coming to the knowledge or attention of the agencies. The damage caused may be irreparable.

If this "cuckoo" is known as a sex offender, there is no problem in tracking him down. If the individual has been identified as a "potentially dangerous offender", then this can be addressed within the Multi-Agency Public Protection Scheme (MAPP) or child care procedures. But if the individual does not fit into a suitable category, then he (or she) could easily, and regularly does, slip through the net.

By initiating a national register, maintained by the police, along with the social services, an intelligence tool for tracking and monitoring these potentially serious offenders would be in place. This would then ensure that there are some safeguards to protect vulnerable children. I am not aware of any existing legislation that could fulfil this requirement.

ii) The medical perspective

Dr Jean Price MB, BS, D.Obs, RCOG, DPH, DPM, FRCPCH, Consultant Paediatrician, Southampton City Primary Care Trust

1. Introduction

A criminal act may have been committed when a child dies under suspicious circumstances, and therefore one could argue that this is a specific problem for the police, lawyers, and judges. However, society needs to find ways to understand why crimes occur and attempt to find other ways of reducing their number. This has particular relevance to health and social services. These deaths consume a large number of resources and have a major impact on family functioning. Child deaths usually occur at times of stress within the family. Factors that contribute to stress include mental health problems, poverty and domestic violence, alcohol and drug abuse. These factors have been highlighted in the various reports of serious case reviews (Part 8 investigations (DH, 2002))[1]. Psychiatric disorder was found in a third of the cases reviewed (Falkov 1996[2]); Domestic violence was found in families of 49 out of 105 children reviewed by Brandon and Lewis in 1996[3]. But it is also known that trying to identify families at high risk and where children are likely to suffer harm is virtually impossible and false positives may be identified.

The power of the individual indicators to predict life-threatening events is limited. Nevertheless, services can be put into place to help families, and the health service can contribute at all levels: at the point of identification of risk (although communication between professionals and agencies is a problem)[4]; at diagnosis, with treatment of both children and adults when they are ill; and in prevention. All young children have contact with health professionals, particularly health care, and therefore the identification of risk and trauma should be feasible, and preventative services put in place.

Health professionals have an interest in working with social services in identifying and ameliorating those factors within a family that make children vulnerable to risk. It is important to identify what the vulnerabilities may be in those unfortunate families where a child has suffered a subdural haemorrhage (SDH), as there may be the potential for harm occurring to others in the family if nothing is done to help. The health and wellbeing of all children must be secured. This can be achieved by being sensitive to, and having the willingness to explore and confront the stresses, strains, violence, illness and addictions of parents. Parents need to be looked

[1] Learning from past experience, a review of serious case reviews, *Department of Health, June 2002.*

[2] *Falkov, A.* A study of Working Together 'Part 8' reports: fatal child abuse and parental psychological disorder. *Department of Health, 1996.*

[3] *Brandon, M and Lewis, A,* Significant harm and children's experiences of domestic violence, *Child & Family Social Work (1996) 1 (1): 33-42.*

[4] The Victoria Climbié Inquiry – Report of an Inquiry by Lord Laming, *January 2003, The Stationery Office.*

after and cared for, as healthy families make healthy children, but we should never put adults' needs before the welfare of a child.

2. Research findings

Domestic violence is a major indicator of child abuse. Three out of every five children suffering abuse (physical, neglect, or emotional) had mothers who were experiencing violence from their partners. Professionals have been noted as giving little attention to the fact that children were witnessing such high levels of violence (Farmer and Owen 1995).[5] Traditionally, the abuse of women and that of children has been examined and managed separately by the various agencies. It is now well recognised that it is not just the acts of violence that produce the harm to the individual woman. The psychological effects of living with the fear and threat of possible violence often have a greater impact on her health and her identity. There is a growing body of research to show that witnessing violence to their mothers can have a detrimental impact on children, tantamount to emotional abuse:

> *"Two decades of empirical research indicate that those children who witness domestic violence are at increased risk of maladaption" (Kolbo, Blakely and Engleman, 1996).*[6]

Children may not actually see the abuse of their mother, but will overhear incidents and be aware of the results and consequences. It is obvious that domestic violence has a major impact on the mother's own emotional wellbeing and will inevitably influence her ability to parent and protect her children.

Domestic violence has also been an important factor in some highly publicised child deaths, including Maria Colwell in 1974 and Sukina Hammond, Toni Dale and Kimberley Carlisle in the 1980s. In these cases there appeared to have been a failure on the part of the services to appreciate the danger that the men in the household represented to the children (O'Hara 1994).[7]

It was not until the 1990s that the links between domestic violence and child abuse were made[8]. Yet, even today, health professionals still receive scant, if any, training on domestic violence. They will rarely confront it, even if it is staring them in the face, as they often feel helpless and are unaware of the services and resources that can be of help to these families.

Since the NSPCC 'Back to Sleep' campaign in the early 1990s, the incidence of Sudden Infant Death Syndrome (SIDS) has fallen markedly. This means that a higher proportion of sudden infant deaths and sudden unexpected deaths of infancy may be due to some form of untoward event, for example by smothering, poisoning or shaking.

The Leeds Inquiry into infant deaths[9] found that of 37 unexpected deaths, six had signs of

---

[5] *Farmer & Owen*. Child protection practice: private risks and public remedies. *The Stationery Office.*

[6] *Kolbo, Blakely and Engelman,* Children who witness domestic violence: a review of empirical literature. *Journal of Interpersonal Violence (1996) 11 (2): 281-293.*

[7] *O'Hara, M.* Child deaths in the context of domestic violence: implications for professional practice, in children living with domestic violence, *Whiting & Birch, London.*

[8] Messages from Research. *Department of Health, 1995.*

[9] *Hobbs C & Wynne J, Leeds Inquiry into Infant Deaths: the importance of abuse and neglect in sudden infant deaths. Child Abuse Review (1995) 4: 329-339.*

abuse. These included a cigarette burn, petechiae (small blood blisters) on the buttocks or chests, graze to the ear, retinal haemorrhages, bruising to the neck, blood in the mouth, genitalia or bladder, and rib fractures in a surviving twin. Of these 37 children, 27 had features of neglect and the other 10 raised serious causes for concern[9]. Neglect is one aspect of abuse that we jointly do not address well or thoroughly enough, probably due to the lack of resources. The thresholds are therefore set too high.

We also appear to take scant notice of the re-abuse of children that are returned to their families. South Wales has an incidence of physical abuse in babies of 114/100,000 each year. 69 babies were examined over two years. Fourteen had been removed from home and one had been re-abused during a contact visit. Of the 49 children who were returned home, 15 (31%) of these experienced further abuse. (Sibert[10]).

Of those children who present to hospital as seriously ill or dead, some do die of natural causes, including SIDS. But those that we are concerned about may have been shaken, poisoned or smothered.

3. Statistics

Incidence of Subdural Haemorrhage in children under two years:

	BPSU (UK and NI)[11]	**Jayawant (1998)[12]**
Under 2 years	12.54/100,000/yr	12.8/100,000/yr
Under 1 year	24.1/100,000/yr	21/100,000/yr

Incidence of Subdural Haemorrhage in children under 2 years as a result of possible shaking:

Under 2 years: 10.13/100,000/year (Jayawant, 1998[12])

Clinical outcome is poor (Jayawant et al, 1998)[12]:
* Nine of 33 infants died (27.3%)
* Another 15 of the 33 infants were disabled (45.5%)
* Nine of the 33 were reported as normal at one year after the event.

NB Bonnier (1995)[13] reported late consequence of 'whiplash shaking injury' in the form of speech and language delay, hyperactivity and learning difficulties. Haviland[14] also reported poor

---

[9] *Ibid*

[10] *Sibert, Professor J, University College of Wales – awaiting publication.*

[11] *BPSU Study – presented at National Conference, British Association for the Prevention of Child Abuse and Neglect, York, July 2003 (awaiting publication).*

[12] *Jayawant et al, Subdural Haemorrhages in Infants: Presentation Based Study. BMJ (1998) 31: 1558-61.*

[12] *Ibid*

[12] *Ibid*

[13] *C Bonnier; M Nassogn; P Evrard, Outcome and Prognosis of Whiplash Shaken Infant Syndrome: late consequences after a symptom-free interval, Dev Med Child Neurol, (1995) 37: 943-956.*

[14] *Haviland, J & Russell R I, Outcome After Severe Non-Accidental Head Injury, Arch Dis Ch (1997) 77 (6): 504-507.*

outcome for children suffering a non-accidental head injury.

Presentation

Jayawant's study showed variable presentation:

- Four of the 33 (22.2%) were dead on arrival
- A total of 20 (60.6%) required intensive care because of fitting, shock or unconsciousness
- Six (20%) had several admissions before diagnosis was made, e.g. with drowsiness, lethargy, off feeds, failure to thrive.

Investigations of those live children (29):

- All live children had blood clotting studies
- A total of 27 (81.8%) had skeletal survey, including three at post mortem
- A total of 24 (72.7%) had ophthalmoscopic examination, only 14 by ophthalmologist.

Conclusion:

- 22 (66.7%) had full basic investigations.

Evidence of co-existing traumatic injury

Thirteen out of the 33 (39.4%) showed other clinical evidence of abuse (torn frenulum, burns, bites, bruising and salt poisoning. This low figure has also been reported by Price[15], when she described only 50% of those with subdural haemorrhage thought to be due to non-accidental injury as having bruising. These bruises are mostly on the face and head and can be quite minor.

Previous abuse in index child or siblings

- Four of the 33 (12.1%) had suffered previous abuse – all died
  Of the 33 children, 17 had siblings:
    - six siblings (35.3%) – previous abuse
    - two siblings (11.8%) – concurrent abuse.

Alexander[16] reports that 71% of shaken infants had evidence of previous abuse. He also makes the point that shaking is NOT an isolated event. Alexander also discussed the severity of the forces needed to cause the injuries seen in shaken babies. He feels that the only other conditions that might mimic the forces are:

a) a major road traffic accident where there will be significant evidence of impact to the skull and probably good witnesses to the event

b) falls from great heights, but Chadwick et al[17] found that only one in 117 children died from

---

[15] *Price, J.* Bruising in Shaken Babies: how obvious is it?, presented at the *European Conference on Shaken Baby Syndrome, Edinburgh, May 2003.*

[16] *Alexander, R. C. et al.* Serial Abuse in Children who are shaken, *American Journal of Diseases in Childhood. (1990) 144 (1): 58-60.*

[17] *Chadwick et al:* Deaths from Falls in Children: how far is fatal? *J Trauma. (1991). 31(10):1353-5.*

a fall from the 2nd, 3rd or 4th storey. In contrast, 20–25% of children die from a shaking injury.

Recent research suggests that infants, who die as a result of shaking, may have evidence of injury to the nerves at the cranio-cervical junction. Geddes et al[18] talked of neuropathological findings in 53 dead children with probable inflicted head injuries. The authors emphasised the whole brain being exposed to hypoxic-ischaemic injury (lack of oxygen and blood) as a result of damage to the tissues in the brain stem (base of the brain). This they thought was the most important insult in these dead children. They had little evidence of damage to the axons (nerves) elsewhere in the brain.

They extrapolated from this that such injury may not be caused by a violent shake.[18]

These findings are seen in a small number of dead children and should not be extended to apply to all other surviving children who have suffered subdural haemorrhages. The authors did not use any radiological images to support their claim.

Kemp[19] however did find that those children with subdural haemorrhages from shaking who presented with anoxia were more likely to have a poor outcome.

4. The role of the health professional

The well being of the child is paramount and forensic interest must never put this in jeopardy. Our interests must be for this child, his or her siblings, and the family as a whole. The presenting seriously ill or collapsed child must immediately receive all the medical care necessary. This may mean that an initial good and comprehensive history is not taken, and a superficial examination for bruises and other injuries does not occur.

However, medical history is very important. Care and time needs to be taken over this, either initially, or at a later date. Social history and previous health of the child and the carers should be noted. Questions should be asked in an open-ended way, for example: "When was he last completely well?" and "Tell me everything that has happened since that time". Any obvious injuries should be pointed out and the parents asked for an explanation: "Are you aware of this bruise?" Usually, each parent will be spoken to separately. At this stage, clinical findings and explanations need to be factual. For example: "We are worried about pressure around the brain". Any spontaneous comments or explanations need to be carefully documented.

It is advisable that the acute paediatrician or neurologist involves a paediatrician with child abuse expertise as soon as possible, in order for child protection procedures to be instigated. This would involve a multi-disciplinary strategy discussion at an early stage in order that a planned investigation can occur.

Parents will need to be introduced to the idea that non-accidental injury may have occurred or

---

[18] *Geddes, J., F. et al.* Neuropathology of Inflicted Head Injury in Children. I. Patterns of brain damage. *Brain. (2001) 124 (7):1290-8. Geddes JF, et al,* Neuropathology of Inflicted Head Injury in Children. II. Microscopic Brain Injury in Infants. *Brain. (2001) 124 (7):1299-1306.*
[18] *ibid*
[19] *Kemp, A., M.* Investigating Subdural Haemorrhage in Infants. *Arch. Dis. Child. (2002) 86 (2):98-102.*

is being considered. The strategy discussion should help to decide when this should occur, who does it and who else should be present. The police will interview parents formally. The home environment may need to be searched by the police, sooner rather than later, in order to secure any relevant evidence that will be helpful.

Once this child has been stabilised medically, a forensic medical examination needs to occur, looking for signs of neglect, bruising, bites, burns, a torn frenulum or bruising to the mouth. The genitalia also need to be examined for damage and any signs of bony injury need to be looked for.

- It may be necessary to take forensic swabs from possible bites, love bites or of any discharge. All samples should be dealt with in a truly forensic way, taking note of the chain of evidence
- All bruises and other injuries should be marked on body maps
- Photographs of all injuries, with appropriate L shaped measuring scales, should be taken (using forensic or hospital photographers). These may need to be repeated, as injuries change over time.

Investigations

Blood

Blood should be taken for bleeding disorders and haemoglobin levels. A low haemoglobin can be an indication of a bleed having occurred some hours previously. Biochemical tests can also be done to check for damage to internal organs, for example, the liver, kidney or pancreas, as can occur with shaking or direct blows to the abdomen. Drugs or poisoning with salt may also need to be investigated.

Urine

This should be collected to look for drugs and for glutaric aciduria, a condition also known to cause subdural haemorrhages[20]. This is associated with atrophy of the brain, which can be detected on a CT scan.

Radiology

This is probably the most helpful to both the medical care of the child, the diagnosis and possible the ageing of the insult, and so helps with the timing of a possible shaking injury. Jaspan[21] and colleagues suggest a protocol be followed which includes serial imaging.

i. Skeletal survey

This is carried out to look for fractures to any bones of the body, particularly the ribs and metaphyseal fractures of the long bones. These can be subtle and sometimes difficult to

---

[20] *Morris, A et al:* Glutaric Aciduria and Suspected Child Abuse. *Arch. Dis. Child. (1999) 80(5):404-5.*

[21] *Jaspan, T. et al.* Neuro-imaging for Non-Accidental Head Injury in Childhood: a proposed protocol. *Clinical Radiology (2003) 58: 44-53.*

visualise, even by an experienced radiologist. It may be helpful to have dual reporting in highly suspicious cases. Metaphyseal fractures are often symmetrical and do not cause pain. They can only be detected on X-ray.

Because of the difficulty in identification of rib fractures, it is recommended that the skeletal survey is repeated in 10 to 14 days to pick up healing, i.e. new bone formation. This would also identify any area of the body that has been damaged previously[22,23,24] and assist with timing of the original injury. All such X-rays should be reported on by paediatric radiologists, but these are not always available in every hospital.

Rib fractures have been described as occurring in five – 27% of children experiencing shaking or shaken impact injury.[25] They are virtually diagnostic of child abuse.

ii. CT scan

This should be carried out at the time of presentation[21] whenever a head injury is suspected. A neuro-radiologist with an interest in paediatric trauma should read the X-rays. CT scans provide good information about an acute (fresh) bleed, skull fractures and soft tissue injuries to the head. It is recommended that this should be repeated within 10 –14 days, when it will help with diagnosing secondary brain damage, possible expansion of subdural haemorrhage or early hydrocephalus.[21]

iii. MRI scan

An MRI scan is ideally carried out within one week of admission. Jaspan would recommend day three – four[21]. This helps to identify older bleeds, ischaemic injuries to and bleeds within the brain tissue as well as bleeds between the hemispheres and in the posterior fossa (at the back of the brain). Such scans can also help identify injury at the cranio-cervical junction, but MRIs are not available in every hospital. Jaspan would also recommend a repeat MRI at two – three months if early injury showed a parenchymal (brain tissue) injury or there was a persisting neurological deficit.[21]

iv. Radio isotope bone imaging

This could help with the diagnosis of rib fractures and possible spinal injuries, by showing up as hot spots. This type of X-ray requires someone with specific skills and is not always available.

Osteogenesis imperfecta is frequently quoted as an alternative diagnosis to child abuse[26].

[22] *Carty, H. Fractures Caused by Child Abuse. J. Bone & Joint Surgery. (1993) 15 (6): 849-857.*

[23] *O'Connor, J., F. & Cohen, J. Diagnostic Imaging in Child Abuse, ed. P Kleinman, Williams & Wilkins. Baltimore 1987:112.*

[24] *Kleinman, P. Follow On of Skeletal Surveys in Suspected Child Abuse. Am. J. Roentgenol. (1996) 167:893-6.*

[25] *Kleinman, P. Skeletal Trauma: general considerations, diagnostic imaging in child abuse, ed. P Kleinman, Williams & Wilkins. Baltimore 1987, 1987a:10, 1987b:67.*

[21] *Ibid*

[21] *Ibid*

[21] *Ibid*

[21] *Ibid*

[26] Albin et al, Differentiation of Child Abuse from Osteogenesis Imperfecta. *Am. J. Roentgenol. (1990) 154:1035-46.*

There are four types of osteogenesis imperfecta. Types II and III usually have very severe bone disease and are therefore easily diagnosed. In mild forms of Type I, fractures do not usually occur before the child starts to walk, whereas with subdural haemorrhage from child abuse, fractures are frequently seen in children under one year.

In the more severe forms of Type one, the children have osteoporosis, wormian bones and blue sclera (which can easily be detected on skeletal survey). Fractures are usually of the mid-part of the long bone (diaphyses). Type IV is very rare and only a few cases have been reported[26].

Bruises

Bruises anywhere on the body are only seen in 50% of cases[15] and mostly on the face and head. Dating bruises is notoriously difficult and is an inexact science. The only colour that gives any indication of age is yellow, which does not appear to be seen before 18 hours after the injury.[27]

Ophthalmology

Retinal haemorrhages and other damage to the eyes are well-recognised injuries in shaken babies. They are seen in 63-85% of cases[12]. Identifying these requires some skill and they may only be visible towards the front of the attachment of the retina within the eye lens. This examination requires indirect ophthalmology and is best done by an ophthalmologist, who is skilled and trained in this method of examination. She/he should also pick up other damage, such as retinal folds and detachment of the retina. Retinal damage and other damage to the eyes can occur in severe accidental injuries and Terson's Syndrome. However, they are much more likely to be seen in child abuse.[28]

Follow-up

Should these children survive, they should be followed up with appointments for neurology, hearing, vision, and long term follow up for more subtle damage such as speech and language problems, hyperactivity and learning difficulties[13].

If these children die, or are brought to hospital dead, they still require a very thorough examination with all the appropriate investigations including a skeletal survey for possible causes of death[29]. The Home Office pathologist and coroner should be provided with as much information as possible on the child's birth and development and any illnesses experienced up to the time of the presentation, along with information on all family members and any concerns there may have been about them. They will need all the information on any investigations carried out. It would be usual for the paediatrician examining the child at the time of death to be involved in this process.

[26] *Ibid*

[15] *Ibid*

[27] *Langlois, N. E. & Gresham, G. A. The Ages of Bruises: a review and study of the colour changes with time, Forensic Sci Int (1991) 50: 227-238.*

[12] *Ibid*

[28] Ophthalmology Child Abuse Working Party. *Eye [1999] 3-9.*

[13] *Ibid*

[29] *Green, M. A. A Practical Approach to a Suspicious Death in Infancy: A Personal View, J Clinical Pathol. (1998) 51: 561-3.*

5. Health Professionals can contribute to the criminal investigation by:

- Carrying out a good and thorough medical assessment[19]
- Taking an initial good and careful history of the child's life and family circumstances
- Providing interpretation of any injuries with dating if possible
- Implementing blood and urine investigations to eliminate other possible causes
- Carrying out investigations may help with the ageing of injuries, eg:
  i initial low haemoglobin indicating early blood loss
  ii the level of drugs within the blood or urine may provide this information
  iii Skeletal survey with a repeat in 7-10 days
  iv +/- an MRI may help with the ageing of subdural haemorrhages
- Paediatric pathologists should carry out post-mortems (but these are a very rare breed)
- Much of what we do to protect children depends on the identification of their needs. Communication and sharing of information is crucial for this to be effective[4]. This needs to be done at an early stage and can pose problems for GPs, either through lack of knowledge or a reluctance to share information with other professionals because of confidentiality issues.

Initial recognition of a subdural haemorrhage from a possible shaking injury can be a problem for those in primary health care and some specialists, even paediatricians. There is still fear and anxiety at pointing the finger at others, particularly if the parents are also under the care of the same G.P. or the alleged offender is a fellow professional. There is also fear among professionals about the possibility of appearing in court, the disruption that this can and does pose to one's professional life, and about the increasingly litigious era in which we live. We are now having great difficulty in recruiting people to work with children and particularly in those posts that have a child protection responsibility.

Sharing information poses particular problems for primary care, because of issues around confidentiality. The Department of Health, the Department of Education and Skills (DFES) and the General Medical Council (GMC) all have a role to play in giving very clear, consistent and unambiguous messages to all professionals working in the field of child abuse. It looks possible that this may come about as a result of the Laming Inquiry.

Fear is best dealt with through education, understanding, peer support and joint working. The Royal College of Paediatrics and Child Health, in conjunction with the NSPCC, is now making robust efforts to develop good training programmes. Its Joint Statement with the Association of Police Surgeons[30], makes it clear that a two doctor examination is a way forward, and registration with the Council for Registration of Forensic Practitioners (CRFP) will give doctors credibility for their presentation of evidence within the courts.

Hopefully in the future, health professionals will work more effectively in helping other agencies and the law to bring about effective change in the management of children who may have suffered a shaking injury.

---

[19] *Ibid*

[4] *Ibid*

[30] Guidance on Paediatric Forensic Examinations in Relation to Possible Child Sexual Abuse *Royal College of Paediatrics & Child Health and The Association of Police Surgeons, April 2002.*

iii) The social services perspective

Andrew Webb, Director of Social Services, Cheshire County Council

1. Introduction

1.1 Social services departments are not routinely a primary partner in the investigation of unexplained or unexpected deaths of children. In many cases they are not even informed of a death unless there are concerns about surviving siblings or they are known to have had substantial prior involvement with the family. As a consequence, the social services contribution to the early stages of investigation and case management is limited and dependant wholly upon a decision by police or health professionals, who are universally involved, to notify them. If this paper addressed only those cases in which children died at the hands of a parent it would have been relatively short and straightforward. However, as the work of the "Which of you did it?" (WOYDI) working group progressed it became clear that these cases needed to be considered as part of a continuum. This includes other unexplained deaths, serious injury from which the child survives, and the long-term emotional harm caused in some families. This position was supported by a survey of 49 area child protection committees (ACPCs) carried out in 2001 by the author (Andrew Webb) as part of the WOYDI project to identify the volume of cases with WOYDI features. The survey found that the numbers of such cases were relatively small but the respondents agreed that many of the issues raised in those cases were similar to those in other child homicide or serious injury cases that had not led to death. Furthermore, comparison with the study carried out by the Association of Chief Police Officers (ACPO) at the same time suggested that as few as one third of child homicides investigated by police forces might have been referred to ACPCs. From a social services perspective this has led to the development of an argument for improving inter-agency reporting and investigation of all cases of child death, serious injury and neglect. If there are improvements in the quality of investigation of all cases, the number in which it is impossible to differentiate between two possible perpetrators should fall.

1.2 Broadening the remit of this paper to include a wider group of unexplained deaths and injuries is not without risk, as it increases the number of extraneous factors that have to be considered. The first of these is the connection with other unexplained deaths, many of which are thought to be due to natural causes. It has been suggested that the best witness in WOYDI cases would have been the victim, but in the case of infants even surviving victims will only be able to give their story through the collection of physical evidence and forensic techniques. The timely collection of the best evidence when a child dies unexpectedly presents a major challenge for police and medical staff. A life-threatening episode or sudden death in an infant, particularly in the absence of obvious trauma, neglect or a prior history of abuse, requires thorough investigation. At this time of acute stress and grief parents and other family members must be treated with respect and sensitivity rather than with a presumption that they are implicated in the death. Improved investigation will lead, it is argued, to a greater capacity to separate suspicious deaths from those resulting from natural conditions; and where maltreatment is the cause, to differentiate between two possible perpetrators. This in turn will lead to a higher conviction rate, which would greatly facilitate progress in any consequent civil proceedings. However, while an inability to identify which of two carers injured a child does not present the same problems to a civil court as to a criminal court it creates as big a challenge to a social services department carrying out a risk assessment and creating a coherent care plan.

1.3   A review of some of the more widely reported WOYDI cases reveals that it is not unusual for a number of agencies to have been heavily involved in supporting the family prior to the final injury. Despite a range of concerns having been expressed over time in these cases, and injuries and incidents of harm noted, insufficient evidence existed to prompt a statutory intervention. This lack of action did not simply relate to an inability to identify which parent might have caused the harm, it also related to the ability to prove that a threshold of harm had been crossed. The threshold of harm may be crossed by a single incident; it may only be reached through the systematic collection and collation of small pieces of evidence. In such a case there is little guidance on what constitutes a critical mass of evidence, particularly when the family circumstances and adult partners change with a degree of regularity. However, once it has been determined that the threshold has been crossed, the ability to differentiate between a safe and a dangerous parent has longer term consequences for social services departments than for those agencies involved primarily in investigation and prosecution. An infant disabled as a result of maltreatment can remain in the care of the social services department through to adulthood; uncertainty about the risk posed by one or other parent can create significant problems over such long periods, particularly when contact or revocation proceedings are launched. Changes in the law or other procedural improvements in WOYDI cases would be supported by social services departments if this led to improved conviction rates or delivered "better" justice. However, such improvements might not have a significant impact on the lives of many survivors of abuse, as social services departments tend to be relatively successful in care proceedings in such circumstances.

1.4   Much of the above relates to the general difficulties in care planning for abused children and really merits a paper in its own right. However, to return to the focus of the debate in respect of WOYDI cases, it is useful to consider the social services role under three separate headings:

- Investigation
- Managing proceedings
- Child protection systems

2. Investigation

2.1   The survey of ACPCs referred to earlier indicated that less than a quarter of the committees that replied had agreed an inter-agency investigation protocol to cover unexplained or unexpected deaths. Of those, only four believed their protocol contained sufficient detail to ensure that medical or paramedical staff were informed of the need to protect evidence when dealing with the presentation of a dead or seriously injured infant. When thinking about a typical case, faced with an unexplained death, the response of the police will depend very much upon the degree of suspicion of the medical personnel about the injury or cause of death. Even when there is suspicion of maltreatment, not all police forces will involve their specialist child protection officers from the outset, preferring to rely on their experienced criminal investigation staff. However, a criminal or murder investigation which is managed as an isolated incident runs the risk of overlooking vital contextual information which might have been supplied by child protection or interagency investigation methods. The history of child death case reviews is littered with examples of personnel in a range of agencies failing to take account of information held by others. There is no reason to believe that the development of a case after a death should be significantly different in this respect from the management of a case in the community.

2.2 It has been noted that the greater the amount of contextual information, the greater the likelihood of turning specific medical or forensic data into useful information. If evidence is collected and interpreted single-mindedly in order that it might be presented in a criminal court then it can be argued that it will be of the highest quality. However, there is a danger that in pursuing and retaining evidence solely for the purpose of prosecution that supportive or "softer" evidence will be missed. Secondary evidence can be invaluable in preparing a case for a civil court or in determining a course of action in respect of subsequent children and as such will be absolutely vital for a social services department in the longer term. Such evidence might range from physical evidence that would be inadmissible in a criminal court through to an analysis of a power relationship between two partners and their reaction in hospital or under police interview. In any event, evidence that is not found and protected at the time of the initial investigation - and for this to happen the primary investigators need to be aware of its possible importance - it is likely to be lost for all time. However, successful outcomes do not always hinge on forensics. Investigation methods developed in family assessments can have a place in WOYDI cases. For example, there can be few more complex dynamics in a relationship than those underpinning a partner's decision to cover up the murder of her/his own child. Joint interview techniques and an understanding of the wider social and cultural forces at play can make a major difference to an investigation in such circumstances. Whether alternative approaches are used to interview a sibling who might be a witness, or to bring an understanding and sensitivity to the issues of domestic violence, it is argued that inter-agency working can pay dividends both in developing the investigation and in the future management of the outcome.

2.3 In addition to using a broader approach to obtaining evidence, more thought needs to be given to using that which already exists. For example, if an investigation is made aware of a longstanding inter-agency involvement in a family it might profit by reviewing existing records. A well-maintained child protection plan would include evidence from a number of professional perspectives, over a period of time. The potential to include "similar fact" evidence to a criminal investigation should not be discounted – whether or not this is later admissible in proceedings.

3. Managing proceedings

3.1 The main thrust of the current debate in relation to WOYDI cases relates to criminal proceedings and it is important to find a way for justice to be done in such complex matters. However, the fate of children involved - whether siblings of a murdered child or a baby born (if not conceived) after the event - can be influenced as much by the process of justice as the outcome. The survey of ACPCs reported above indicated a wide variation in practice by the police and Crown Prosecution Service (CPS). In some cases an early decision not to proceed was taken by the investigating officer or his or her senior officer.

While this did not necessarily aid decision-making in respect of the approach to be taken by social services to proceed in a civil court or to provide family support, at least a decision had been taken which made planning possible. In a number of cases the decision not to proceed was taken at a very late stage. In others, the case went all the way to trial only for no evidence to be offered. In these circumstances the problems faced by the social services department can become extreme, particularly if the presumptions underpinning the care plan included the removal of both parents. Although it is the subject of a national debate in its own right, delay in civil proceedings must also be considered in this context. The scale of delay in some cases becomes damaging to a child, and is compounded by a decision not to use the same evidence in a criminal court that is being relied upon in the civil court. Such a decision opens up a whole new set of arguments for a parent who is determined to contest an order - and in WOYDI cases there is a good chance that 50 per cent of such parents have committed no act of abuse. Fortunately the survey results indicated that the civil courts had relatively few problems making orders in these circumstances but this does not mean that the subsequent care planning was straightforward. Creating stable, permanent placements for children is hard enough but when faced with the possible threat of an "innocent" parent applying for contact or a revocation it becomes that much more difficult. It would also appear from the ACPC survey that a number of the cases reported had been resolved by the use of kinship placements. History informs us that the capacity of a parent who has not been convicted of harm and is at large in the community to undermine such placements is potentially very high.

3.2   The ACPC survey also indicated that decisions not to proceed with criminal cases were taken in isolation by the police and the CPS rather than following consultation. Whether such decisions might have been changed by the inclusion in debate of the viewpoint of other disciplines cannot be known. However, it does seem reasonable when so much can depend on both the timing and outcome of a decision in respect of the criminal matters, that the requirements of other agencies should be incorporated into the process. It is not clear whether the recent pilot approach to the joint management of civil and criminal proceedings by a single judge would have had an impact in cases such as these. However, it can be argued that better communication should be expected as a matter of course and that the multi-agency case conference should become a feature of planning for both criminal and civil proceedings.

3.3   The ACPC and ACPO evidence of a low rate of "completion" of WOYDI cases in criminal proceedings would be even more worrying if this were the only route available to protect children. Nevertheless, the pragmatic use of civil law appears to be capable of compensating in cases in which surviving siblings require protection. However, social services departments regularly work with families in which the composition changes or, in which it can be argued that circumstances have changed since a major issue of abuse was investigated. In such cases the absence of a previous conviction can present a major evidential hurdle to new proceedings.

4. Child protection systems

4.1   As a lead agency in an ACPC, it is incumbent upon social services departments to ensure that procedures and inter-agency practice reflect the latest developments in thinking and that lessons are learned through case reviews. Public confidence in child protection systems is also of major importance if communities are to be successfully encouraged to take more responsibility for the safety of their more vulnerable members. Although there has been tremendous progress in working together in the child protection system over the past decade, there is still major public concern that the systems do not work well enough. The media seizes upon every incident of poor professional communication or apparent lacuna in the law to support this view. ACPCs have a part to play at a local level in addressing the image of the child protection system and encouraging the public to report their concerns.

4.2   Additionally, ACPCs have a duty to ensure that interagency procedures are effective and that lessons learned from practice or case review are disseminated in the professional community in their area. The Department of Health (DH) has a duty to ensure that this happens nationally. It is clear from the ACPC review reported above that neither level can claim significant success in this field. For example, of the 19 ACPCs that carried out a review of a case with WOYDI features, none felt it had developed a model of good practice (this has subsequently improved). Additionally, decisions about legal processes were seen as inconsistent and unpredictable yet ACPCs were not reporting any action they had taken to rectify this in a way that would have national impact. Despite public reporting of WOYDI cases, ACPCs have been slow to share the results of any reviews they have carried out, and the DH has not, to date, published a review of the findings of local case reviews that might inform practice in this area.

4.3   If the key agencies' public response to the death of a child in WOYDI cases is restricted to a powerless shrug of the shoulders and an attempt to explain the legal loophole, then what hope do they have in addressing some of the grey areas of child maltreatment?

5. Recommendations

The survey of ACPCs carried out and the interdisciplinary discussions that have been a feature of the WOYDI working party process have led me to conclude that the following developments would lead to an improvement in "case management" for a wider working group of abused children. They would also help those involved in WOYDI cases:

- A common, national inter-agency protocol for the investigation of unexplained and unexpected deaths in children should be developed and published

- A national system of reporting such deaths should be created and research commissioned to identify trends and to identify best practice in their investigation

- The DH should commission specific research into existing serious case reviews to ascertain whether there are issues requiring immediate action either for ACPCs or specific agencies in the child protection system

- A national protocol for the management of parallel civil and criminal proceedings should be introduced to both improve the quality of risk analysis in specific decisions and to reduce delay in civil processes.

iv) The academic perspective

Professor John R. Spencer, Selwyn College, University of Cambridge

1. Sometimes a young child is intentionally injured in the home and cannot say who did it – either because he is too young, or because the injuries prevent him. Where there were two adult "carers", of whom either or both could have inflicted the injuries, the law at present makes it difficult to convict either of them of any criminal offence. This problem is well known to the NSPCC, to the police, and to anyone else who is involved in the task of investigating serious offences committed against children.

2. The law on the subject stems from a series of reported cases that have appeared in the law reports over the last 15 years. The main ones are:

   Lane and Lane (1987) 82 CrAppR 5; child of 22 months, killed by the effects of a single blow; parents convicted at trial of manslaughter; manslaughter conviction quashed because of uncertainty as to which one was present when the blow was struck; qualifying the earlier case law (particularly Gibson and Gibson (1985) 80 CrAppR 24) the Court of Appeal held that, in such a situation, the prosecution has failed even to establish a case to answer; cruelty convictions under S.1 CYPA 1933 were upheld for related injuries in respect of which there was other evidence.

   Russell and Russell (1987) 85 CrAppR 388; 15-month-old child, killed by administration of methadone; distinguishing Lane and Lane, the Court of Appeal upheld the conviction; in this case, there was evidence that both had been involved in doping the child with methadone in the past, and this, it said, made a crucial difference.

   Aston and Mason (1991) 94 CrAppR 180; both carers prosecuted for murder of 16-month-old child, apparently killed by throwing or battering her against a hard surface; conviction for manslaughter at trial; conviction quashed because there was no clear evidence as to which parent was present when the fatal injury was inflicted, and – applying Lane and Lane – this meant there was **not even a case to answer**.

   Strudwick and Merry (1994) 99 CrAppR 326; child of three killed by two heavy blows to the abdomen; both parents convicted of manslaughter at trial – conviction quashed for same reason as in Lane and Lane and Aston and Mason. But the Court of Appeal upholds convictions for child cruelty on the basis of other injuries ("long-term cruelty"), relating to which there was other evidence.

   S and C [1996] Criminal Law Review 346; an 18-month-old child suffers a series of assaults over a period of three months and "a number of serious and horrifying injuries" during a period of 19 hours. Convictions at trial for grievous bodily harm and child cruelty; convictions quashed applying Lane and Lane, Aston and Mason, etc.

3. Taken in the round, they seem to establish the following propositions:

   i. A conviction for murder, manslaughter, wounding or assault is impossible if the prosecution cannot establish which one, or ones, of the child's parents were present when the injuries were inflicted; nor is it possible to convict for child cruelty, if this is based on deliberately hurting the child as against failing to seek medical attention. In this situation, the law says that there is not even a "case to answer". (Unless, that is, there is some further piece of legally admissible evidence - like a confession, or perhaps evidence of previous assaults which can be attributed to one or other of the parents.)

ii. If it can be shown that one parent, and one alone, was present when it happened, and that parent can be identified, there is a case to answer, and a reasonable prospect of conviction.

iii. If it can be shown that both parents were present at the time the injuries were inflicted, there is still a problem if it remains unclear which one of them did it; although in such a situation the chances of conviction are higher, because it is sometimes possible to argue "joint enterprise". That is, if parent A did it, parent B must have helped, either actively or by wilfully failing to intervene when he/she could have done so, and vice versa.

iv. If, after the child was injured the child needed medical attention and was not given it, it may be possible to convict either or both parents of child cruelty on the basis of their failure to provide the child with medical treatment - provided it can be shown that the parent in question knew that the child was sick. Irrespective of which one initially hurt the child, both are under an obligation to seek medical help. (See, for example, S and M [1995] Criminal Law 486.)

4. This state of affairs is widely believed to be unsatisfactory because it is said to result in persons who have committed serious offences against defenceless children escaping justice. How far this is really so, and if it is, whether it is feasible to do anything about it, are both contentious matters. However, it is worth examining at a theoretical level what the current legal obstacles to conviction are, and what would be involved in removing them.

5. The following appear to be among the major legal difficulties in such cases:

i. Where the prosecution cannot establish which one, or ones, of the child's parents was/were present when the injuries were inflicted, there is not in law "a case to answer". In consequence the trial never reaches the stage at which the parents either enter the witness-box and get asked awkward questions by the prosecution, or alternatively refuse to enter it - when their refusal to explain themselves at trial is likely to treated as a piece of evidence against them under the Criminal Justice and Public Order Act 1994 s. 35.

ii. The parents' blanket refusal to explain themselves to the police in such a situation does not, as such, amount in law to a piece of admissible evidence against them. Under the Criminal Justice and Public Order Act 1994 it may do so in certain circumstances, in particular where the parents give evidence at trial and give an explanation which, if true, they might reasonably have been expected to give to the police; but obviously this situation does not arise if (because of (i) above) the trial never reaches the point where the parents give evidence.

iii. Evidence of bad character (e.g. a proved general tendency to violent assault) is generally inadmissible as evidence.

6. Any or all of following changes would probably make it easier to obtain convictions in these cases. All of them are contentious - and a number of them I do not myself support.

i.   Reversing the rule that where you are one of two parents or carers of a child who suffers non-accidental injury, there is "no case to answer" unless it can actually be shown that you were present at the time the injury was inflicted. This change would have the practical effect of "smoking out" the defendants in these cases and (in effect) forcing them to give evidence and submit themselves to cross-examination: as a result of which it might in some cases become clear what actually happened. Speaking as one who does not rank the right of silence particularly highly, I think this would be desirable. However, it is open to the objection that, if no further evidence did come out, the defendants would be at risk of a conviction on the basis of insufficient evidence. As against this, it is possible to point to a number of other situations where, for policy reasons, the courts have set the threshold of "a case to answer" very low. For example, the mere fact of being found in possession of recently stolen goods amounts to a prima facie case of handling – and perhaps more pertinently, the mere fact of being identified as part of the crowd constitutes a prima facie case of various public order offences. (See Allen v. Ireland (1984) 79 CrAppR 206.)

ii. Altering the rules about what evidence is legally admissible in such a case, so that all or any of the following potentially count against the defendants (see the appendix to this paper, below):

(a) Refusal, in such a case, to give an explanation to the police.
(b) Evidence of bad character – in particular, a tendency to violence. (At present, the prosecution can use as evidence previous assaults this defendant has committed against this particular victim – but (as a rule) not assaults against other members of the family.)
(c) Evidence of what one parent said against the other when questioned by the police. (At present, statements made to the police are admissible against the maker as "confessions" – but they are not admissible against other people. In the UK this position is usually defended – but it is not the position in a number of other countries.)

iii. Change the law to require the parents, in such a situation, to give an explanation when questioned by the authorities. Make their refusal punishable as a criminal offence, and also make their answers admissible against them at a subsequent trial for an offence against the child. (Surprisingly, Parliament has adopted this drastic technique on a number of occasions in the past where various forms of financial crime were concerned. But it is contrary to Article 6(1) of The European Convention on Human Rights (ECHR) as interpreted by the Strasbourg Court – and cost the UK a condemnation at Strasbourg in the Saunders case in 1997.)

iv. Provide, by law, for a reversal of the onus of proof – so that the law says (in effect):
"Where you were one of the carers of a child who suffers non-accidental injury, in any prosecution for an offence of injuring the child you are presumed to have been involved unless you can persuade the court that you were not."

(This is another drastic technique that Parliament has frequently adopted in other contexts in the past. A prominent example appears in the offence of aggravated vehicle taking. However, if the offence in question is severely punishable, the technique seems to be contrary to Article 6(2) of the ECHR, which protects the presumption of innocence. See the House of Lords decision in Lambert [2001] 3 WLR 206.)

v. Create a special offence of being one of the carers of a child who suffers non-accidental injury; for which you have a defence if you can show that you were not actively involved in inflicting the injury yourself, nor negligently failed to prevent it. (Making a criminal offence out of the existence of suspicious circumstances is another drastic technique that Parliament has frequently adopted in the past. Striking examples are S.4 of the Explosive Substances Act 1883, and S.16 of the Prevention of Terrorism (Temporary

Provisions) Act 1989. But where the offence is severely punishable, the technique is open to the same objection as the one described in the previous paragraph.)

Appendix to Professor John Spencer's paper

Evidence of previous violence

In outline, the present law can be stated as follows:

The fact that the accused has a criminal record may not be used in evidence against him, nor any other evidence that merely shows he has a tendency to commit an offence. However, evidence which incidentally reveals the defendant's bad character is admissible, provided it shows something else that is more directly relevant as well. Thus evidence of bad character (or criminal convictions) is not admissible if it merely shows that the defendant is someone who is likely to break the criminal law; nor even where it shows that he has a tendency to break this particular part of it; but it is admissible, although it happens to show this too, if it also shows his guilt by some other and more direct chain of reasoning.

Although the rule is not difficult to state in abstract terms, it is often exceptionally difficult to apply. It is one thing to say that such evidence is admissible wherever it shows something more than a mere criminal tendency, but quite another to say whether this condition is met in any given case, because in practice the matter is often not clear-cut but rather a question of degree. In consequence a large and ever-spreading body of case law has grown up around it, interspersed with several difficult statutory provisions. The result is a lot of complex law.[1]

In a case where a parent or caregiver is prosecuted for killing or injuring a little child, when would a court currently admit evidence revealing the defendant's violent tendencies as showing more than "mere tendency" and being "directly relevant"?

The paradigm case where "similar fact evidence" (as it is usually called) is admissible is where a series of different people make similar complaints against the same defendant. Where the complaints are all so similar that their simultaneous concoction would be an extraordinary coincidence, the courts admit evidence of all the complaints in order to reinforce their individual effect and to suggest that the defendant is a repeat offender with a particular *modus operandi*.[2] This situation arises quite often where defendants are accused of sexual offences against children. In the nature of things, however, it does not arise where children have been killed, or very little children killed or injured. In these cases, the victim is in no position to make a complaint, and the cases on similar complaints are not relevant.

According to a related line of cases, "similar fact evidence" would in principle be admissible where the defendant had previously been involved in a series of incidents, each one of which might plausibly have been an accident when viewed on its own, but the totality of which presents a compelling case that the defendant caused all of them deliberately. The celebrated "Brides in the Bath" case is an example.[3] Another is the case of Makin[4], where the bodies of dead babies were found buried in the gardens of a series of houses, all of which had been occupied by the defendants, who were accused of "baby-farming".

---

[1] *In the current edition of* Cross and Tapper on Evidence *its exposition takes up 104 pages (of a 800 page book).*

[2] *DPP v P [1991] 2 AC 447.*

[3] *Smith (1915) 11 CrAppR 229.*

[4] *Makin v A-G for New South Wales [1894] AC 57.*

According to another group of cases, evidence of the defendant's previous violent behaviour is also in principle admissible if it shows not merely a general tendency to use violence, but a tendency to use it against one particular victim. The Court of Appeal has so held in the most recent cases[5], and has justified this by reference to a general rule that the court is entitled to hear "similar fact evidence" wherever it is necessary to understand the general background to the case.

Where it is necessary to place before the jury evidence of part of a continual background of history relevant to the offence charged in the indictment and without the totality of which the account placed before the jury would be incomplete or incomprehensible, then the fact that the whole account involves including evidence establishing the commission of an offence with which the accused is not charged is not of itself a ground for excluding evidence.[6]

The matter is not entirely clear, however, because in earlier cases the courts held otherwise. In *Mackie* (1973) 57 CrAppR 453, for example, where a father was prosecuted for the manslaughter of a three-year-old boy who had fallen downstairs when running away from him, the Court of Appeal was unhappy that the trial court had heard evidence that the defendant was in the habit of hitting him. The Court of Appeal said that the evidence was admissible to show that the child was frightened of the defendant, but seemed to think it was not admissible to show that the defendant had a tendency to knock the child about. It is possible, if perhaps unlikely, that at some point the earlier case law will be resurrected.

What is clear beyond doubt, however, is that as the law stands it would not be permissible to use as evidence against a parent or caregiver charged with a child's unlawful homicide the fact that he or she had a general tendency to violent behaviour. Nor would such evidence be admissible, it seems, even if the previous violence was specifically directed against children.[7]

Two years ago, the rules relating to "similar fact evidence" were relaxed to some extent by the decision in R v Z.[8] Here the House of Lords ruled that, in a situation in which "similar fact evidence" is admissible in principle, it can be used even where the "similar facts" led to an attempt to prosecute the defendant which resulted in acquittal. Thus, for example, if a parent were prosecuted for murdering his child, the prosecution could now use as evidence of guilt the fact that he had previously assaulted the child, even if he had been prosecuted for the alleged assault and at trial acquitted. Although important, the scope of this new decision is quite limited. Whilst allowing evidence of "similar facts" to be admitted notwithstanding an acquittal at the time, it does not otherwise expand the type of evidence that can be used.

In practice the theoretically strict exclusionary rule is sometimes circumvented, either officially or unofficially, by other legal rules:

- First, if the defendant defends himself at trial by attacking the prosecution witnesses, he can then be cross-examined about his bad character if he is then foolish enough to go

---

[5] *Williams (1987) 84 CrAppR 299; c.f. Fulcher [1995] 2 CrAppR 251.*

[6] *Pettmann (1985) (unreported), quote with approval in Fulcher (previous note).*

[7] *Wright 90 CrAppR 325. The case decides that, on a charge of sexual offences against children, evidence is not admissible to show that the defendant, when charged with buggery on youths, had a propensity to commit buggery with males. The same would apply, a fortiori, to evidence showing a tendency to abuse them violently.*

[8] *[2000] 2 AC 483.*

[9] *Originally S.1(f) (ii), and renumbered by the Youth Justice and Criminal Evidence Act 1999.*

into the witness box. This is because the Criminal Evidence Act 1898 S.1 (3) (ii)[9] expressly so provides. In such a case, the defendant can in principle be cross-examined about his bad character generally – and not merely those aspects of it that the prosecution could, exceptionally, use as part of the case against him. Thus it could, for example, cross-examine him about his general tendency to violent behaviour.[10]

- Secondly, the strict exclusionary rule is circumvented to some extent by the rules relating to *joinder*, the rules about where the defendant can be tried for several difference offences simultaneously, or tried together with other people.

Under the rules governing the trial of joint defendants, if one defendant tries to put the blame on his co-defendant, the co-defendant is entitled to respond by cross-examining him about his bad character – including, where relevant, his tendency to violence.[11] In addition, and independently of this, where two defendants are jointly accused of a violent offence, one of whom has a record for violent behaviour and other of whom does not, the one with no record for violence is allowed to defend himself (or herself) by calling evidence about the violent record of the other.[12]

The rules governing when the defendant can be tried for more than one offence also allow the rule on "similar fact evidence" to be circumvented, but this time unofficially. In the crown court, the defendant may be tried for more than one offence in a single trial where these offences are "founded on the same facts, or form or are a part of a series of offences of the same or a similar character"[13]. As interpreted by the House of Lords,[14] these rules make it possible for a defendant to be tried for a series of offences that are broadly similar, notwithstanding the fact that the evidence on one count is not formally admissible under the "similar fact evidence rules" to prove the defendant guilty of the other. Thus, for example, a defendant who was accused of assaulting two different children on two separate occasions could be tried for both at once, and the jury would learn from this that the prosecution believed neither incident to be a "one-off". In theory, the jury in such a situation is of course expected to disregard the evidence on each count when deciding whether the defendant is guilty of the other. But in practice, the fact that the jury hears the evidence undermines the strictness of the rule against "similar fact evidence".

If there are some factors that tend to relax the rule, there are other important factors pulling in the opposite direction.

The first is that, even where evidence of bad character is in principle admissible, the trial judge has discretion to exclude it.[15] In practice some judges are particularly reluctant to admit it, and most defendants try to persuade judges to suppress this sort of evidence in cases where the prosecution tries to use it. Although the Court of Appeal is usually reluctant to quash a conviction merely because it disagrees with the way the trial judge chose to exercise one of his discretionary powers, it sometimes does so. Prosecutors are aware of this and some, anxious to make sure that the conviction, if there is one, is "appeal-proof", chose not to call this type of evidence in cases where they could. Thus the rules excluding "similar fact evidence"

---

[10] *E.g. Marsh [1994] Criminal Law Review 52, where under this provision a defendant prosecuted for assault committed on the rugby field was cross-examined about his disciplinary record for violent play.*
[11] *Criminal Evidence Act 1989 S.1 (3) (iii) (formerly S.1 (f) (iii)).*
[12] *Lowery v R [1974] AC 85; Bracewell (1978) 68 CrAppR 44.*
[13] *Indictment Rules 1971, Rule 9.*
[14] *Ludlow v Metropolitan Police Commissioner [1971] AC 29.*
[15] *R v H [1995] AC 596.*

undoubtedly have a "chilling effect", leading to this type of evidence being suppressed, even where the rules theoretically permit its use.

The "chilling effect" is undoubtedly enhanced by the fact that the rules, as we have seen, are abstruse and complicated. Not only do prosecutors and judges sometimes voluntarily suppress evidence tending to reveal the defendant's bad character, knowing that it is theoretically admissible, but "similar fact" evidence is probably sometimes suppressed because the rules, being complicated, are misunderstood.

The usual reason for the rule suppressing evidence of bad character and tendency is said to be:

> "the exaggerated importance that a jury, consisting of persons without legal experience may attach to this kind of evidence; for they may argue: 'this man is charged with crime, and the police think he did it, and he is clearly of criminal habits; therefore he must be guilty'."[16]

How far this is really so is open to debate. There is no doubt that evidence of the defendant's previous misconduct makes courts more willing to convict, but this is not the same as saying that it makes them more willing to convict persons who are innocent. However, assuming that the rule suppressing evidence of bad character is generally a sound one, we think that there is a strong case for admitting evidence of a tendency towards violent behaviour against a defendant who is accused of killing or injuring a child in his care.

In its recent White Paper *Justice for All*, the Government proposes a relaxation of the "similar fact evidence" rules, and as an example of how its proposed approach would work in the context of domestic violence, gives the following:[17]

> "The defendant is charged with assaulting his wife. He has a history of violence, including a number of convictions for assault occasioning actual bodily harm, and there are witness accounts of him striking his wife in the past. He claims that she received her injuries falling down the stairs. In this case, his previous conduct could be thought relevant to determining whether the allegations of violence, or the defendant's version of events, are true. The judge should therefore be able to rule whether this is admissible, provided that he is satisfied that it can be put in its proper context by the jury."

The NSPCC's "Which of You Did It?" working group believes that this approach is also right in the related context of the ill-treatment and neglect of little children.

The real risk with this sort of evidence is not so much that the court will give it disproportionate weight, but the risk of its being used as a substitute for other and more cogent evidence in a case where there is really nothing else. This is not the situation where the defendant was one of two persons who were looking after a child, and it is they and they alone who had the opportunity to inflict the injuries as a result of which it died.

---

[16] *Glanville Williams.* The Proof of Guilt *(3rd ed. 1963) p.214.*
[17] Justice for All, *Cm 5563 (July 2002), p.80.*

v) The defence perspective

Christopher Kinch, QC

1. The conventional view of the Bar has been that we are dealing with a small minority of cases where this problem leads to the failure of a prosecution. There has also been a feeling that there are other courts, where the interests of the child are paramount, where inferences as to who is responsible may more readily be drawn. The view is summed up in the quote from Lord Goddard:

    > *"Although it is unfortunate that a guilty party cannot be brought to justice, it is far more important that there should not be a miscarriage of justice and that the law should be maintained rather than that there should be a failure in some particular case."* (R v Abbott (1955) 39 Cr App R 141 (at p148)).

2. It has to be acknowledged that the figures available to this working party show that there is a much greater problem. It prevents many cases from even reaching the stage where the prosecution advocate applies his or her mind to the prospects of securing a conviction. The defending advocate's position must be that possible solutions to the problem should not include a watering down of the standard of proof in cases where a child is the victim.

3. These are very difficult cases in which to defend. It is the professional duty of the defending barrister to "endeavour to protect his client from conviction except… upon legally admissible evidence sufficient to support a conviction for the offence charged". There is no reason for the defending advocate to concede any diminution in his efforts on the grounds of the nature of the offence or even the fact that the victim was a defenceless child. There can be little doubt that the current state of the law may encourage defence lawyers to adopt a "defensive strategy", aiming to ensure that the prosecution does not obtain evidence from the defendants that might point to a way out of the "Which of You Did It?" dilemma.

4. The defender has to see a prosecution as the action of the State against the individual. In that contest, the State has all the resources at its disposal. It decides the pace of the investigation, at least in the early stages. It has first choice of expert assistance and so on. The defence has to react at every stage, increasingly under great pressure of time in relation to obtaining authority for expert evidence and getting the evidence itself, along with access to an expert who may be able to assist in unearthing errors in the prosecution approach. Defence advocates are wary of the concept of the single "court" expert.

5. The defending advocate has a horror of presumptions, adverse inferences and reverse burdens of proof. He (or she) will do everything he legitimately can to contest their application in any particular case. Human rights legislation is on his side. There is a particular difficulty in advancing an argument based on adverse inference in a case where there are two carers. Inferences should only be drawn where there is no reasonable explanation for silence other than guilt. In the sort of case we are considering there will almost invariably be at least one other possible explanation for silence, namely the wish to avoid blaming the partner who is also under suspicion. The defending advocate is on weaker ground resisting

evidence of previous violence where the prosecution can make it relevant. Spontaneous utterings to neighbours or ambulance men are also hard to counter.

6. There are three areas that provide room for reform and possible improvement:

    i. **Evidence Gathering**

        In the past, many cases have failed because key evidence was unavailable or was not looked for. It is essential that protocols for accident and emergency staff, ambulance staff, police and social services emphasise the importance of recording and retaining evidence. Spontaneous utterances, responses to enquiries, photographs, clothing, all need to be considered.

    ii. **Case Preparation**

        There must be a rigorous examination of the evidence before a suspect is charged. It is not every case of this type that needs fall into the category of "two possible suspects, no conviction". It is important that the evidence should be examined in the context of the case against each defendant individually. It may be that the evidence better supports a case against one rather than both carers. Historical evidence should not be overlooked. There may be a pattern of behaviour that can be relied upon, drawn from available records. It may be that alternative charges such as Attempting to Pervert the Course of Justice should be considered in a particular case.

        There is also a need to ensure that prosecuting advocates are kept up to date on the relevant forensic and medical issues. The Criminal Bar Association (CBA) will play its part in assisting with education programmes.

    iii. **Law Reform**

        The idea of imposing a duty on a carer to provide an explanation in the case of serious injury to a child or death needs careful consideration. Such a duty would doubtless have to be defined with great care. Concern at the potential erosion of an adult's right to silence might be outweighed by a sensible appreciation of the responsibilities undertaken by someone who becomes a parent or carer. The use, in a trial, of answers obtained under compulsory powers would however lead to opposition and problems. What is to be done about the carer who refuses to answer: will that refusal give rise to an adverse inference?

        Whether or not the "duty to explain" sees the light of day, the next proposal is just as controversial. It has been suggested that hearsay statements made by one carer could become evidence against the other. Here we are considering answers given by one carer in an interview under caution in the course of which he or she blames the other carer for the violence.

        This is a proposal that risks offending against many advocates' notion of a fair trial. It is not just that it may be impossible to challenge the allegation in cross examination but that there will often be a strong interest on the part of the maker of the statement to deflect blame onto the other carer. Defending advocates have to recognise that the law must be equipped with sensible ("Strasbourg-proof") means of discovering the truth. They will look to see strong safeguards built in to any such proposals.

        The decision of the Court of Appeal in Lane and Lane (1987) 82 CrAppR 5 (see above) is regarded as responsible for preventing many cases from reaching a jury. The problem with simply reversing the decision is that there is a risk of simply delaying the point at which the nettle is grasped. If neither carer gives evidence how is the jury to be sure of guilt unless a lower standard of proof is brought in through the back door for this type of offence? The intimate pressures and strains on a defendant facing trial with his or her partner impose an additional layer of concerns when facing the choice of giving evidence or not.

There is no doubting the gravity of the problem. The issues merit serious debate and the Law Commission's interest in this area of the law is to be welcomed.

7. Reflections on Sentencing

7.1 The maximum sentence for Cruelty to Children (the offence under the Children and Young Person Act 1933 S.1) was increased to 10 years' imprisonment for offences committed after 29 September 1988. Previously, the maximum sentence had been two years. The increase in sentence reflected public concern at the prevalence and disturbing nature of these offences. The section is very widely drawn, with the result that there is a vast range and variety of offences to consider.

7.2 A review of the sentences in cases reported in the sentencing encyclopaedia and elsewhere suggests that after 1988 the courts began to impose sentences well in excess of the previous maximum in serious cases of cruelty. More recently the courts have been prepared to impose sentences in the region of eight years' imprisonment for the worst cases. It is worth noting the example of the Tracy Wright case in Norwich. His Honour Judge Mellor took the view that the appalling cruelty inflicted by the defendant before the child died had to be reflected by a consecutive sentence. As a result he sentenced Wright to 10 years for manslaughter and a further five for cruelty. The Court of Appeal took the view that 15 years was too long in total and varied the sentence to 12 years for the manslaughter, making the five years for the cruelty run concurrently.

7.3 An argument raised on a number of occasions by appellants in cases of child cruelty is that the long sentence imposed was out of line with sentences for manslaughter. Putting it crudely the argument is to the effect that "I would have got a lesser sentence if the child had died so this sentence must be excessive". Fortunately, the Court of Appeal does not appear to have been persuaded by this argument as it is usually dealing with a case of appalling suffering on the child's part. However, it is a feature that underlines the importance of prosecuting authorities being aware of appeals against sentence and offering or even seeking to be present to assist the court. The prosecution is involved in the sentencing process to a much greater degree than ever before. It can be argued that the prosecution's absence from most appeals against sentence is illogical. The question of whether sentences for manslaughter are too low is another matter.

7.4 There remain two areas of concern. The first is whether the maximum sentence for cruelty should be revisited once more. The argument runs that, where judges feel constrained to pass sentences very close to the maximum in bad cases, there ought to be some "headroom" for the worst cases. Another way of looking at the point is to consider not just the scale of injuries inflicted but the overall damage caused to the children concerned. Taking that perspective, it can be argued that the victims of the worst cases of neglect and cruelty suffer in a way that parallels the suffering of victims of offences of wounding with intent and inflicting grievous bodily harm with intent. Ought the maximum sentence to be increased to life imprisonment to reflect that position?

7.5 The second concern is that there exists a degree of unevenness in the range of sentences passed. There has been no guideline case and there are no plans for the Sentencing Advisory Panel to look into sentences for cruelty at the moment. Guidance would be welcome on issues such as the identification of aggravating features, the proper weight to be placed on the length of the conduct, the effect of the mental and emotional capacity of the defendant.

Sentencing in cases of cruelty, summary table

YEAR	CASE	CHARGE	SENTENCE
1990	Lowther	GBH with intent to baby	8 years
1991	AG's ref #13	GBH with intent + cruelty: baby 7 wks	6 years
1993	Drake	GBH with intent: baby 3 months	4 years
1993	Emery	Cruelty: baby 11 months	30 months
1994	David	Cruelty: young baby	3 years
1995	Banu & Ali	Wilful neglect	3 years
1996	Pikesley	GBH with intent: child 13 months	4 years 4 months
1996	J	GBH and cruelty: child 6 yrs	8 years
1997	Bricklebank	GBH with intent: child 2 yrs	5 years
1998	Scammell & Mills	Wounding and cruelty: child 21 months	6 years & 7 years
1998	M	Cruelty to 3 children	3 years
1998	Weaver and Burton	Ill-treatment and wilful neglect: child died at 15 months	3 years & 2 years
1999	Adams and Sherrington	Cruelty x 3: child 15 months	7 years & 4 years
1999	Taggert	Cruelty: child 3	30 months
2000	Creed	Neglect	5 years
2001	Brown	GBH and cruelty	3 years
2001	Webb	Manslaughter + cruelty: baby daughter	5 years
2001	Yates	Manslaughter: daughter 3 months Suggests range is 2 to 5 yrs with more for sustained cruel conduct	5 years (reduced from 7)
2001	Bustin	Manslaughter and cruelty	10 years (7 years concurrent)
2001	McWilliams	Cruelty	8 years
2001-2002	Wright	Manslaughter and cruelty	10 years & 5 years consec. Reduced to 12 years
2002	Brereton	Cruelty: single incident of neglect, child died	3 years reduced from 4

NB: Cruelty to persons under 16: (Children and Young Persons Act 1933, S.1) ten years maximum if the offence was committed on or after September 29, 1988, otherwise two years (CJA 1988 S.45).

Cruelty to person under 16, where offender interested in any sum of money payable on death of person under 16: (Children and Young Persons Act 1933, S.1(5)) five years.

There are no guideline cases.

vi) The prosecution perspective

Alison Kerr, Chief Crown Prosecutor, Lincolnshire

1. Introduction

1.1 Cases involving death or serious injury to young children where it is not possible to say which of two parents was responsible for the injury present particular difficulties for the prosecution. The law is well settled and is set out in some detail in Professor Spencer's paper. Generally speaking they are in no different position to any other defendant save that they have a duty to intervene in the ill-treatment of their child by the other parent.

What must be proved?

- Both actually participated in the assault, or
- One assaulted the child whilst the other actively encouraged the assault, or
- One assaulted the child whilst the other, knowing what was happening, failed to intervene to protect the child. This allows an inference that the other was aiding or abetting or there was joint enterprise.

1.2 The possible scenarios are:

(a) The child suffers a serious injury and it is impossible to establish which parent inflicted the injury or that both were present and could have intervened, and medical help is sought immediately, a prosecution for the substantive act, murder or manslaughter will not succeed. Prosecuting both parents for neglect is not an option since there is no delay in seeking medical assistance.

(b) If there is a failure to seek medical assistance in the above scenario a prosecution for neglect can be considered on the basis that each is under a duty to intervene to protect the child.

(c) If the child suffers a series of non-accidental injuries and it is not possible to establish which parent inflicted the injuries, a prosecution of both parents for neglect can be considered.

1.3 These scenarios can be challenging enough for the prosecution but they can be more complicated. Examples might be:

(a) A child suffers non-accidental injury where a mother has sole care of a child and there is a casual boyfriend who does not have responsibility for the child within the meaning of S.1 of the Children and Young Persons Act 1933. Again it is not possible to establish who has inflicted the injury. Proceedings for neglect can only be considered against the mother if she has failed to seek medical help. Sometimes, if the casual boyfriend has inflicted the injury she may start by shielding him and then later change her mind. The difficulty then is that she may no longer be considered to be a credible witness.

(b) A child suffers non-accidental injury and other carers have been involved, for example grandparents or babysitters. This can be particularly challenging if there is only a single incident leading to death or serious injury.

1.4 Cases of this nature may fail at a number of different stages:

- They may be referred to the Crown Prosecution Service (CPS) to advise pre-charge and advice is given that there is insufficient evidence to proceed
- They may be referred to the CPS post-charge and advice is given that there is insufficient evidence to proceed
- They may fail during the prosecution process.

The CPS does not keep specific figures on the failure of these cases. A possible way forward may be a joint thematic review by HM Crown Prosecution Service Inspectorate and HM Inspectorate of Constabulary to analyse reasons for failure and to identify good practice. (Similar to the recent joint thematic review of rape cases.)

2. The extent of the problem

2.1 To inform the working group all Chief Crown Prosecutors were asked the question:

> *"Can you indicate how many cases have been referred to your area in the last three years where cases have either not been commenced or have failed on the basis that there has not been sufficient evidence to say which of the parents/carers have caused death or serious injury?"*

The responses were based on the recollections of those dealing with the cases but they reflect and support the police figures and the extent of the problem.

2.2 Suffice to say that these cases are given very careful consideration and are generally dealt with by specialist lawyers. It has for some years now been the policy of the CPS to require that lawyers dealing with child abuse cases should have received appropriate training. This means that lawyers build up experience in dealing with these cases.

3. Improving the way in which these cases can be prosecuted

3.1 Chief Crown Prosecutors were also asked:

> *"What can be done within the existing law to bring about a successful prosecution, with particular regard to the investigation and the prosecution process?"*

- All that responded stressed the importance of early involvement by the CPS and also the early involvement of prosecuting counsel. There were concerns that premature decisions might be made which could not be rectified. For example, whether a partner is to be treated as a witness or a defendant. In particular some felt that there should be no charging of the defendant before there is full medical evidence and advice from the CPS and, if necessary, counsel. The recent charging pilots where the CPS has been responsible for the decision to charge have highlighted the benefits of pre-charge advice.

- The background and overall picture are necessary. If there are previous incidents of violence, these should be investigated and information provided for the reviewing lawyer. This should include relevant inquiries into medical records and possibly social services records. This is not a licence to go on a "fishing expedition" but under the Criminal Procedures and Investigations Act 1996, the police have a duty to pursue all reasonable lines of inquiry which can include investigation into third-party material. There are issues around consent to access medical records and any issues involving public interest immunity would have to be properly addressed. Many areas now have protocols dealing with third party material and public interest immunity.

Much of this is addressed in the Sussex Joint Agency Protocol: *Unexplained Child Deaths* (see Appendix).

In Andrew Webb's paper dealing with the social services perspective there is a reference to the need for communication between agencies and for the sharing of information. This is particularly relevant where there are proceedings under the Children Act 1989 and relevant evidence has been obtained. This can include medical reports. Currently this evidence cannot be released without the order of the court.

Some prosecutors have experienced difficulty when Children Act proceedings have preceded the criminal prosecution. It was generally considered that in such serious cases the criminal prosecution should if possible take precedence.

- Specialist police officers and CPS staff, who have received appropriate training, should handle cases. This could include, in addition to training on law and evidence, awareness of the likely cause of injuries and the research findings, which correlate various factors with increased likelihood of death, or serious injury to very young children. These have been shown to include domestic violence, drug and alcohol abuse. Many counsel have built up a degree of expertise in these cases and have previously dealt with some of the complex medical issues

- There was a perceived shortage of forensic experts, particularly pathologists who are able to provide detailed and specific conclusions. There was also a concern about how to identify and deal with unreliable experts

- The prosecution should provide the defence with the expert medical and forensic evidence at the earliest opportunity to enable them to seek an expert opinion. This should include the disclosure of all relevant information including medical notes. A court hearing may be necessary if there are issues of public interest immunity. The defence practice of failing to disclose their report if it supports the prosecution expert was within the *Crown Court (Advance Notice of Expert Evidence) Rules 1987*. However some prosecutors were unhappy about the practice of using the report to cross-examine the prosecution expert

- Professor Spencer has outlined in some detail the current position with regard to the use of evidence of previous violence and the use of similar fact evidence. From my own experience I would endorse his view that there is a reluctance on the part of prosecutors to seek to use similar fact evidence if there is sufficient other evidence. This stems from a concern that a conviction may then be vulnerable to appeal. On the other hand there can be reluctance on the part of the trial judge to admit such evidence where the case is otherwise weak. A prosecution right of appeal as proposed in the Government's White Paper *Justice for All* (June 2002) would be helpful to enable the prosecution to challenge, in appropriate cases, a ruling to exclude similar fact evidence

- Prosecutors should consider whether it is possible to join a number of charges on the same indictment in accordance with Rule 9 of the *Indictment Rules 1971.* This states:

> *"Charges for any offences may be joined in the same indictment if those charges are founded on the same facts, or form or are part of a series of offences of the same or a similar character".*

In a recent case where I was the reviewing lawyer a request by the defence to sever an indictment which included a charge of murder in relation to one child of the family as well as counts relating to violence against three other children was unsuccessful. The case of R v Christou (G.) (1997) AC 117, HL is helpful, where Lord Taylor CJ reviewed the authorities and stated that the appropriateness of separate trials will depend on the particular facts of each case. The relevant factors will vary from case to case, but the essential criterion is achieving of a fair resolution of the issues. That requires fairness to the accused but also to the prosecution and those involved in it.

4. What can be achieved within the existing case law?

- The facts of the case should be carefully considered against the existing case authorities. These are set out in some detail in Professor Spencer's paper

- The case of Lawson and Thompson C of A 30 July 1993 illustrates that it is possible to build a case by investigating thoroughly the circumstances surrounding the death in conjunction with expert medical opinion as to the time and cause of death. The following were accepted as evidence of the joint participation in the manslaughter of a child:

  - The appellants were the only adults in the house at the time of the injury, which lead to the death of the child
  - They were the only people capable of causing the injury to the child
  - They had a quarrel when both had lost their tempers
  - The child was treated by one appellant in such a way that he screamed for five minutes
  - A neighbour overheard this
  - Both must have been awake at the time
  - Their lies in interview
  - Their lies to paramedics
  - A total of 120 recently inflicted bruises.

From that the court said the jury was entitled to conclude:

  - There was an attack on the child by one of the appellants during which the child screamed for five minutes
  - The other appellant would have heard the screams wherever they were in the house
  - The other appellant must have been awake
  - The other appellant had made no attempt to intervene.

The reason for setting this case out in some detail is to illustrate that it is possible to build a case by investigating thoroughly the circumstances surrounding the death in conjunction with expert medical opinion as to the likely time and cause of death.

5. Would any changes in the law help?

5.1 A number of suggestions have been made which may assist in these cases to a point where, at least the defendants, have to answer the case against them. I will endeavour to give the prosecution perspective. As a prosecutor, however, one must remain objective and ensure that the trial process is fair, no matter how serious the charge.

- **Altering the burden of proof** - by introducing some sort of rebuttable presumption. There was general concern about going down this road. Article 6(2) of The European Convention on Human Rights (ECHR) guarantees the right to everyone charged with a criminal offence to be "presumed innocent until proven guilty according to law". Article 6(2) does not necessarily prohibit the operation of presumptions of law and fact. However, any rule which shifts the burden of proof, or which applies a presumption operating against the accused, must be confined within reasonable limits. There is authority for such reversal of the burden of proof within the ECHR jurisprudence Salabiaku v France (1988) 13 EHRR 379 and RP v United Kingdom (1972) Application No.5124/71 42 CD 135. In Lambert 3 W.L.R. 206 the House of Lords decided that a reverse burden under S.28 of the Misuse of Drugs Act 1971 was incompatible with Article 6 and was not proportionate to the public interest aims that were being pursued. The judgement has wider implications as far as the issue of reverse burden of proof is concerned. In cases where the question is: "Which of two people has caused fatal injuries to a child?", there would generally be no difficulty with establishing that an offence had been committed and that such a provision would be used to deal with a very serious offence in the eyes of society. The issue is: "Which person perpetrated the fatal act or acts or whether both were in some way acting together?" Each would be asked to answer the case even if the prosecution could not establish presence and in circumstances where they would have every motive for blaming each other

- **Use of the defendant's previous convictions or evidence of previous incidents** This should be considered in the light of the proposals in *Justice for All*. This is set out at paragraphs 4.52 to 4.59. At paragraph 4.57:

  > *"Where a defendant's previous convictions, or other misconduct, are relevant to an issue in the case, unless the court considers that the information will have a disproportionate effect, they should be allowed to know about it. It will be for the Judge to decide whether the probative value in introducing this information is outweighed by its prejudicial effect. These safeguards will be set out in legislation. This will reform the current haphazard collection of exclusionary rules."*

  No doubt there will be considerable debate about these proposals

- **Creating an offence imposing a duty on carers to supply information within their knowledge, which carries a penalty for non-compliance**. As Professor Spencer has pointed out, there are instances of this type of provision dealing with less serious matters. The decided cases on the right against self-incrimination, Article 6(1) of the ECHR appear to make a distinction between a single simple question and a prolonged interrogation. Compare the case of Saunders v UK, 23 EHRR 313, where interviews with the inspectors of the Department of Trade and Industry under the Companies Act 1985 were held to violate article 6(1) with those dealing with the duty to respond to a single question as to the identity of the driver under section 172 the Road Traffic Act 1988. In Brown v Stott (2001) 2 All ER 97 it was held that the penalty for non-compliance was a proportionate response to the problem of maintaining road safety. Given the seriousness of the offence and the views of society more than simple questioning may be seen as proportionate. Convention challenges are likely to arise where evidence is obtained using compulsory powers where criminal sanction is available.

6. Allowing the statement of each to have evidential weight against the other

6.1   This was put forward by Professor Spencer who has pointed out that this happens in other jurisdictions. Christopher Kinch QC has commented on this proposal from the defence perspective. It would indeed be helpful to get past the stage of a case to answer but there would need to be adequate safeguards in place.

Appendix

The Sussex Joint Agency Protocol

Unexplained child deaths

Introduction

Why the need for the protocol?

It is important to remember that the majority of unexplained child deaths occur as a result of natural causes and are an unavoidable tragedy.

About one in two thousand children die unexpectedly in infancy and it is unusual for two such deaths to occur in the same family. The incidence of such deaths in children decreases as the child gets older. Professional staff from a number of different agencies will become involved throughout the process of establishing the cause for the death.

A number of child death reviews have highlighted the lack of guidance for professionals in dealing with the unexplained deaths of children. This protocol is not intended to be prescriptive but endeavours to provide guidance to practitioners who are confronted with these tragic circumstances. It is acknowledged that each such death has unique circumstances and each professional involved has their own experience and expertise, which, quite rightly, is drawn upon in their handling of individual cases. Nevertheless, there are a number of common aspects to the management of unexplained child deaths, which it is important to share in the interest of good practice and achieving a consistent approach.

This protocol gives an insight into the priorities of those professionals involved, in an attempt to promote a mutual understanding of each agency's roles and responsibilities. Professionals need to strike a balance between the sensitivities of handling the bereaved families, and securing and preserving anything that may aid them in arriving at an understanding of why the child died.

What is in the protocol?

The protocol contains general advice and guidance in dealing with such deaths along with information concerning inter-agency working. It describes some of the factors that may arouse cause for concern about the circumstances surrounding the death. Finally, there are specific guidelines that provide more detailed information to individual agencies.

The age of child to which the protocol should be applied

The protocol should be applied for children up to the age of 12 years, with discretion for it to be applied to children up to 17 years old.

Principles

When dealing with an unexplained child death all agencies need to follow five common principles:

a) Sensitivity, open mind/balanced approach
b) An inter-agency response
c) Sharing of information
d) Appropriate response to the circumstances
e) Preservation of evidence

NB: All items on this list are equal in importance

1. General advice for all professionals when dealing with the family

1.1   This is a very difficult time for everyone. The time spent with the family may be brief but actions may greatly influence how the family deals with the bereavement for a long time afterwards. A sympathetic and supportive attitude whilst maintaining professionalism towards the investigation is essential.

1.2   Remember that people are in the first stages of grief. They may be shocked, numb, withdrawn or hysterical.

1.3   All professionals must record history and background information given by parents/carers in as much detail as possible. The initial accounts about the circumstances including timings must be recorded verbatim.

1.4   It is normal and appropriate for a parent/carer to want physical contact with his or her dead child. In all but exceptional circumstances, such as when crucial forensic evidence may be lost or interfered with, this should be allowed, albeit with observation by an appropriate professional.

1.5   The child should always be handled as if he/she were still alive remembering to use his or her name at all times as a sign of respect and to preserve dignity.

1.6   All professionals need to take into account any religious and cultural beliefs that may impact on procedures. Such issues must be dealt with sensitively but the importance of the preservation of evidence should not be forgotten.

1.7   The parents/carers should be allowed time to ask questions about practical issues, this includes telling them where their child will be taken and when they are likely to be able to see him/her again.

1.8   Where possible, written contact names and telephone numbers should be given.

1.9   In unexplained child death cases an inquest may be conducted by HM Coroner to establish the cause of death.

1.10 Staff from all agencies need to be aware that on occasions, in suspicious circumstances, the early arrest of the parents/carers may be essential in order to secure and preserve evidence and thus effectively conduct the investigation.

Agency professionals must be prepared to provide statements of evidence promptly in the above circumstances.

Unexplained child death:

The sequence of events

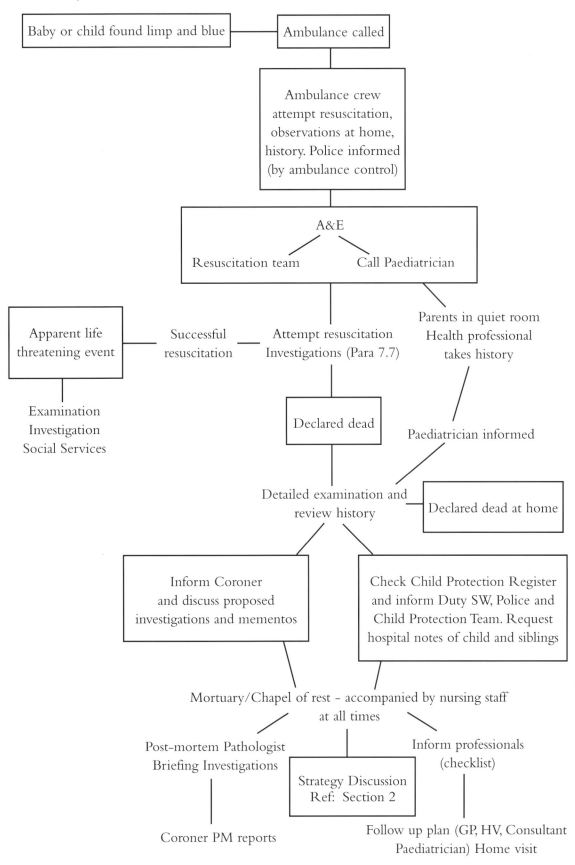

Baby or child found limp and blue — Ambulance called

Ambulance crew attempt resuscitation, observations at home, history. Police informed (by ambulance control)

A&E

Resuscitation team   Call Paediatrician

Apparent life threatening event

Successful resuscitation

Attempt resuscitation Investigations (Para 7.7)

Parents in quiet room Health professional takes history

Examination Investigation Social Services

Declared dead

Paediatrician informed

Detailed examination and review history

Declared dead at home

Inform Coroner and discuss proposed investigations and mementos

Check Child Protection Register and inform Duty SW, Police and Child Protection Team. Request hospital notes of child and siblings

Mortuary/Chapel of rest – accompanied by nursing staff at all times

Post-mortem Pathologist Briefing Investigations

Strategy Discussion Ref: Section 2

Inform professionals (checklist)

Coroner PM reports

Follow up plan (GP, HV, Consultant Paediatrician) Home visit

2. Interagency working

2.1   All unexplained child deaths must be treated as a multi-agency child protection investigation. Surviving siblings may well be the subject of enquiry under Section 47 of the Children Act 1989.

Strategy Discussion

2.2   A strategy discussion will be convened under the child protection procedures as soon as possible and within 72 hours of the child's death. The police officer responsible for investigating the child's death or their representative must be present at this meeting.

2.3   The purpose of the strategy discussion will be:

"For each agency to share information from within case notes/documentation which may shed light on the circumstances leading up to the child's death. This will include the child's previous health, previous child protection issues, previous unexplained or unusual deaths in the family, neglect or failure to thrive, unusual presentations of the child, parental substance misuse etc. This information will usually need to be shared with the pathologist/coroner."

"To enable consideration of any child protection risks to siblings/any other children living in the household and referral within child protection procedures."

"To ensure a co-ordinated bereavement care plan for the family."

2.4   Contribution to the Strategy Discussion will include:

i)   **Health** – the doctor who certified death, the named health visitor for the child, the GP, and representative(s) of the designated health professionals.
ii)   **Social services** – Duty team.
iii) **Police** – Child Protection Team.
iv)   Other contributors may include the **ambulance service** and **education service** (where the child was attending school or nursery).

3. Factors that may arouse suspicion

3.1   Certain factors in the history or examination of the child may give rise to concern about the circumstances surrounding the death. If any such factors are identified, it is important that the information is documented and shared with senior colleagues and relevant professionals in other key agencies involved in the investigation. The following list is not exhaustive and is intended only as a guide.

3.2   **Previous child deaths**
Approximately 1:2000 children die unexpectedly in infancy. Two deaths occurring within the same family is extremely unusual and should arouse suspicion.

3.3   **Previous child protection concerns within the family relating to this child or the siblings**

3.4   **Inappropriate delay in seeking help**

3.5   **Inconsistent explanations**

The account given by the parents/carers of the circumstances of death should be documented verbatim. Any inconsistencies in the story given on different occasions should arouse suspicions, although it is important to bear in mind that some inconsistencies may occur as a result of the shock and trauma caused by the death.

3.6 **Evidence of drug/alcohol abuse** - particularly if the parents/carers are still intoxicated.

3.7 **Evidence of parental mental health problems** - including Munchausen Syndrome or Munchausen Syndrome by Proxy.

3.8 **Unexplained injury, for example, unexplained bruising/burns/bite marks**

It is also very important to remember that a child may have serious internal injuries without any external evidence of trauma.

3.9 **Presence of blood**

The presence of blood must arouse suspicion, although it is occasionally found in cases of natural death. A pinkish frothy residue around the nose or mouth is a normal finding in some children whose deaths are due to sudden infant death syndrome (SIDS).

3.10 **Neglect Issues**

Observations about the condition of the accommodation, general hygiene and cleanliness, the availability of food, adequacy of clothing and bedding and temperature of the environment in which the child is found are important. This will assist in determining whether there may be any underlying neglect issues involved.

4. Agency guidelines

Police: Who should attend?[22]

4.1 It is important for police officers to remember that for most unexplained child deaths, the death has been the result of **natural causes**. Their actions therefore need to be a careful balance between consideration for the bereaved family and the potential of a crime having been committed.

4.2 If the police are the first professionals to attend the scene then urgent medical assistance should be requested as the first priority.

4.3 Police attendance should be kept to the minimum required. Several police officers arriving at the house can be distressing especially if they are uniformed officers in marked police cars.

4.4 Officers should at all times be sensitive in the use of personal radios and mobile phones, etc. If at all possible, the officers liaising with the family, while remaining in contact with colleagues, should have such equipment turned off.

4.5 A detective sergeant must attend the scene. This will preferably be the detective sergeant from the relevant child protection team (CPT). Such officers have the necessary

---

[22] *"Scene" is referred to in this protocol as the child's home. This is assuming that the child died at home and is still there when the police and other professionals attend. However, on many occasions the child will already have been taken to the hospital. If this is the case, the principles remain the same. However, in such a situation, there may be two scenes and resources will need to be allocated accordingly. It is important to note that if the child has already been moved from the home, this does not negate the need for professionals to visit the home.*

investigative skills and knowledge within the field of child protection and inter-agency working.

4.6   If it is not possible for a CPT detective sergeant to attend and the detective sergeant from the criminal investigation department (CID) attends, then the CPT must become involved at the earliest opportunity. If there is no CPT Officer on duty then one should be called out.

4.7   The coroner's officer must be notified as soon as possible. As well as the usual functions he (or she) performs, his experience in dealing with sudden deaths and bereaved families will be invaluable in explaining to the parents/carers what will happen to their child's body and why. It will be extremely useful for the coroner's officer to attend the scene. If the coroner's officer asks to attend the scene then this should be allowed without the necessity of further consultation. He will also be able to liaise directly with the coroner. The investigating officer and the coroner's officer should continue to liaise closely throughout the investigation.

4.8   The detective sergeant will assess the situation and decide on whether it is necessary to immediately consult with a detective inspector, or whether such notification can wait. Some detective inspectors may feel that they wish to be contacted immediately by their detective sergeant in all cases. This will be left to the discretion of each division.

4.9   The senior detective attending will be responsible for deciding on whether to request the attendance of a scene of crime officer (SOCO). Certainly if items are to be removed or photographs or a video are to be taken (see 4.12) then their attendance will be essential.

4.10   If the death is thought to be of a suspicious nature, then a senior investigating officer (SIO) must be informed immediately.

Initial action

4.11   The provision of medical assistance to the child is obviously the first priority. If an ambulance is not already in attendance then one must be immediately requested unless it is absolutely clear that the child has been dead for some time. If this is the case then a doctor will need to be called to certify death. This will be a police surgeon if there are any overt suspicions as to the cause of death.

4.12   The first officer at the scene must make a visual check of the child and its surroundings, noting any obvious signs of injury. It must be established whether the body has been moved and the current position of the infant should be recorded. All other relevant matters should also be recorded (See above). The senior detective attending is responsible for ensuring that this is done.

4.13   An early record of events from the parents/carers is essential, including details of the child's recent health. All comments should be recorded. Any conflicting accounts should raise suspicion but it must not be forgotten that any bereaved person is likely to be in a state of shock and possibly confused. Repeat questioning of the parents/carers by different police officers should be avoided at this stage if at all possible.

4.14   The preservation of the scene and the level of investigation will be relevant and appropriate to presenting factors (see above).

All these are dependent on consideration:

- Commencing a scene log

- General preservation of the scene
- Arranging for photographs of the scene/other rooms, etc
- Retaining bedding but only if obvious signs of forensic value such as blood, vomit or other residues★
- Retaining items such as the child's used bottles, cups, food, medication which may have been administered★
- The child's nappy and clothing remaining on the child but arrangements should be made for them to be retained at the hospital★
- Records of monitoring equipment used by the Ambulance Service that may be of evidential value; it is possible this information may only be retained for 24 hours.

★ See paragraphs 4.15 and 4.16 below

NB. The above is NOT an exhaustive list of considerations and should be treated only as a guide. They will not be necessary in every case. (See above: Factors that may arouse suspicion).

4.15 If it is considered necessary to remove items from the house, do so with consideration for the parents. Explain that it may help to find out why their child has died. Before returning the items, the parents must be asked if they actually want them back.

4.16 If articles have been kept for a while, try to ensure that they are presentable and that any official labels or wrappings are removed before return. Return any items as soon as possible after the coroner's verdict or the conclusion of the investigation. The term investigation will include any possible trial or appeal process.

4.17 Consideration must be given to evidencing factors of neglect, which may have contributed to the death such as temperature of scene, condition of accommodation, general hygiene and the availability of food/drink.

4.18 A G5 Report of Death form must be completed at an early stage. The coroner's officer will complete this if he is in attendance. However, in order to avoid delay, it may be appropriate for an officer to complete the form.

4.19 Questions regarding the child's recent health can be recorded on the G5 under the appropriate heading. These questions should include the basic medical history of the child and family. Other relevant details thought to be pertinent to the child's death should also be included. An example of this could be when the child was last fed.

4.20 The issues of the continuity of identification must be considered. This will preferably be done by the coroner's officer but could be done by a police officer. It should be carried out appropriately and sensitively. The child should be handled as though he/she were alive.

4.21 In all cases where the body is taken directly to a hospital or a mortuary, arrangements must be made for a consultant paediatrician to be informed of the child's death, in order that an appropriate examination of the body can be made.

4.22 If the parents/carers wish to accompany the body to the mortuary, then this should normally be facilitated, ensuring that an officer or coroner's officer accompanies them, as above.

4.23 Police officers need to be aware of other professionals' responsibilities, including resuscitation attempts, taking details from the parents, examination of the dead child and looking after the welfare needs of the family. They may need to wait until some of these things have happened and take details from these professionals before being introduced to the parents. This is where liaison and joint working is essential, as there may be urgent evidential reasons why the police need to take urgent action. It is strongly advised that the CPT be utilised for such liaison wherever possible.

4.24   If it is considered that a skeletal survey may be required prior to the post-mortem, this should be discussed with the coroner so that the appropriate arrangements can be made with the pathologist.

4.25   All families should be visited at home within 24 to 48 hours by a paediatrician or other health professional, liaising with the police officer responsible for investigating the child's death or their representative, to gather information about the baby, family and circumstances of death and to offer initial support.

5. Ambulance staff

5.1   Immediate notification to the police is required by the ambulance service when they are called to the scene of an unexplained child death – this will generally be undertaken by the emergency patient communication centre contacting the police control room.

5.2   The recording of the initial call to the ambulance services should be retained in case it is required for evidential purposes.

5.3   Ambulance staff should follow their national training manual as follows:

(a) Do not automatically assume that the death has occurred.
(b) Clear the airway and if in any doubt about death, apply full CPR.
(c) Inform the accident and emergency department giving estimated time of arrival and patient's condition.
(d) Transport the child to a casualty department or children's hospital if nearer (local arrangements to apply).
(e) Take note of how the body was found.
(f) Pass on all relevant information to the casualty department.
(g) Ensure that any injury is compatible with history.

5.4   The first professional on the scene (e.g. paramedic/GP) should note the position of the child, the clothing worn and the circumstances of how the child was found.

5.5   If the circumstances allow, note any comments made by the carers, any background history, any possible drug misuse and the conditions of the living accommodation. Any such information must be passed on to the receiving doctor and the police.

5.6   Any suspicions should be reported directly to the police and to the receiving doctor at the hospital as soon as possible.

6. General practitioners (GPs)

6.1   There are times when a GP is called to the scene first. In such circumstances they should adhere to the same general principles as for the ambulance staff (see above).

6.2   It is important for the GP to contact the police or coroner's officer if they are the first on the scene (taking into account the primary responsibility of saving life/certifying death). It is advised that the best route for this is to contact the police control room.

6.3   Additional guidance for GPs and health visitors, particularly in relation to the longer term care of the family, can be obtained from two Foundation for Sudden Infant Death publications:

Guidelines for GPs when cot death occurs

Guidelines for Health Visitors when cot death occurs

While these booklets are written specifically for dealing with cot deaths, many of the principles will apply to other child deaths.

7. Hospital staff

7.1   The identity of the people present and their relationship to the child needs to be ascertained.

7.2   If the child is dead upon arrival at the hospital or subsequently dies from an unexplained death, the hospital must immediately check that the police have been notified. Contact should be made with the police area control room where there is 24-hour cover.

7.3   The initial examination and history of the child is extremely important. When the child is brought to the hospital, the consultant paediatrician and A&E consultant should be informed.

7.4   A full general examination should be undertaken by the consultant or paediatric registrar reporting on injuries, rashes and observations about cleanliness of the child, the bedding and the clothing. The examination should include a retinal examination if possible. If any injuries are noted, the police must be immediately informed.

7.5   The detailed history should be obtained as sensitively as possible during resuscitation and as appropriate afterwards. Make detailed records including who is present and what was said.

7.6   The paediatrician should obtain background information including a full medical history, a family history, siblings and a history of any other infant deaths and concerns regarding this incident or previous incidents.

7.7   Prior to death, specimens of blood, urine and other relevant samples can be taken for metabolic investigations, toxicology and to exclude infection. The nature of any tests performed must be accurately recorded for the pathologist. After death, no samples should be taken without prior consultation with the coroner.

7.8   The site and route of any intervention in resuscitation, for example venepuncture or intra-osseous needle, needs to be carefully recorded.

7.9   Personal mementoes should not be taken from the child, nor items of clothing or bedding returned to parents/carers until after the initial investigation is complete, and without prior consultation with the coroner.

7.10   Allow the parents or carers to see and hold their child while accompanied discreetly by a professional.

7.11   Explain to the parents or carers that the coroner has to be informed and that a post-mortem will be necessary to try to discover the cause of death.

7.12   The attending doctor should speak directly to the coroner or coroner's officer.

7.13   Other professionals also need to be informed and this can be done in liaison with the police officer. NHS Trusts will have their own checklist.

7.14   A consultant paediatrician should request and review all hospital records of the child and siblings.

7.15   Health professionals should record parents' or carers' comments in detail in case future discrepancies or suspicious circumstances develop.

7.16   The child's body should not be left unattended until in the mortuary. When the child's body is taken to the mortuary, a professional should be present. It is not essential for the police to undertake the role.

7.17   The consultant paediatrician and the family's GP should together decide on appropriate follow-up.

7.18   All families should be visited at home within 24 to 48 hours by a paediatrician or other health professional, liaising with the police officer responsible for investigating the child's death or their representative, to gather information about the baby, family and circumstances of death and to offer initial support.

Advice for hospital staff in dealing with an unexplained acute life threatening event:

Inform the duty paediatrician who will inform the duty consultant paediatrician.

Review the history of events and carefully record detailed standard paediatric history. A full examination should include features of neglect or injury, a history of similar events, or unexplained child deaths in the family.

Any investigations should address both medical and non-medical causes.

Child protection checks must be initiated for the child and the siblings. Any suspicions must be immediately reported to the social services.

Although these guidelines relate to unexplained child deaths, health professionals must ensure that in the event that of an unexplained acute life-threatening event, the same procedures are followed.

8. Coroner/pathologist – post-mortem

8.1   After the death is certified, the coroner has control of the body and mementoes and medical samples should not be taken without prior consultation.

8.2   The generally agreed principle is that if, after an evaluation of all the facts, there are no grounds for suspecting anything other than a natural death, the post-mortem can be conducted by a local pathologist or paediatric pathologist. If during the post-mortem the pathologist becomes at all concerned that there may be suspicious circumstances, he (or she) must halt the post-mortem and contact a Home Office pathologist.

8.3   If the coroner has any concerns, having been made aware of all the facts, that the death may be of a suspicious nature, then the Home Office pathologist will be used in conjunction with a paediatric pathologist.

8.4   Both the coroner and the pathologist must be provided with a full history at the earliest possible stage. This will include a full medical history from the paediatrician, any relevant background information concerning the child and the family and any concerns raised by any agency. The investigating officer is responsible for ensuring that this is done.

8.5   The coroner's officer must ensure that all relevant professionals are informed of the time and place the post-mortem will be conducted as soon as possible.

8.6   The investigating officer should attend the post-mortem. If this is not possible, then he (or she) must send a representative who is aware of all the facts of the case. A scene of crime officer must attend all post-mortems conducted by a Home Office pathologist. The consultant paediatrician should also be invited to attend.

8.7   The pathologist will arrange a number of examinations at post-mortem. These include a skeletal survey, swabs, blood, urine, bile and gastric aspirate for toxicology, and metabolic investigations.

8.8   If the paediatrician has arranged any similar investigations before death, the coroner must be informed and the results forwarded.

8.9   All professionals must endeavour to conclude their investigations expeditiously. This should include the post-mortem results such as histology. The funeral of the dead infant must not be delayed unnecessarily.

8.10   The interim or final findings of the post-mortem should be provided immediately after the post-mortem examination is completed. The interim result may well be "awaiting histology/virology/toxicology" etc.

8.11   The final result must be notified in writing to the coroner as soon as it is known. The final report should then be sent to the coroner within seven to 14 days of the final result being known.

8.12   When a Home Office pathologist has been used, the pathologist should provide an interim report within two working days of the post-mortem, either orally or in pro-forma. A full written report should be provided to the investigating officer, normally via the coroner, within 15 days of receipt of the exhibited photographs. Where the scientific examination extends beyond 20 days of the post-mortem, the investigating officer should be informed.

8.13   The investigating officer should ensure that a copy is forwarded to the CPT for inclusion on file for future reference. The report must not be shared with other agencies without the permission of the coroner. Permission should always be sought by an agency if the content of the report could potentially affect the agency's future actions. The consultant paediatrician (responsible for the follow up) may request a copy of the post-mortem from the coroner's office. This cannot be released without the coroner's permission.

Further reading and contacts

What Really Happened? Child protection case management of infants with serious injuries and discrepant parental explanations. Peter Dale, Richard Green and Roger Fellows. NSPCC.

Death Certification and Investigation in England, Wales and Northern Ireland: the report of a fundamental review 2003. Cm 5831. The Stationery Office.

Children: their non-accidental death or serious injury (Criminal Trials): a consultative report. The Law Commission (Law Com. No 279). April 2003.

Working together to safeguard children: a guide to inter-agency working to safeguard and promote the welfare of children. Department of Health (DH); Home Office; Department of Education and Employment (DfEE). The Stationery Office, 1999.

Children: their non-accidental death or serious injury (Criminal Trials): a consultative report. The Law Commission (Law Com. No 282). September 2003.

The Foundation for the Study of Infant Deaths

The Foundation for the Study of Infant Deaths has a 24-hour helpline offering support and information to anyone who has suffered the sudden death of an infant.

Helpline number: 0870 787 0554

The helpline is also available for family and friends and those professionals involved with the death. The telephone advisers personally answer the telephone every day of the year.

The Foundation has a wide range of leaflets and information for bereaved families and professionals. It also has a network of befrienders who are previously bereaved parents. Arrangements can be made for a befriender to contact the bereaved family to offer additional support.

FSID General enquiries: 0870 787 0885

References

[1] *Children: their non-accidental death or serious injury (Criminal Trials): a consultative report.* The Law Commission (Law Com. No 279). April 2003.

[2] *Working together to safeguard children: a guide to inter-agency working to safeguard and promote the welfare of children.* (1999). London. The Stationery Office. Department of Health (DH); Home Office; Department for Education and Employment (DfEE):

[3] Lane and Lane (1987) 82 CrAppR 5; child of 22 months, killed by the effects of a single blow; parents convicted at trial of manslaughter; manslaughter conviction quashed because of uncertainty as to which one was present when the blow was struck; qualifying the earlier case law (particularly Gibson and Gibson (1985) 80 CrAppR 24) the Court of Appeal held that, in such a situation, the prosecution has failed even to establish a case to answer; cruelty convictions under s.1 CYPA 1933 were upheld for related injuries in respect of which there was other evidence.

[4] *Children: their non-accidental death or serious injury (Criminal Trials): a consultative report.* The Law Commission (Law Com. No 279). April 2003.

[5] In the current edition of Cross and Tapper on Evidence its exposition takes up 104 pages (of a 800 page book).

[6] DPP v P [1991] 2 AC 447.

[7] Smith (1915) 11 CrAppR 229.

[8] Makin v A–G for New South Wales [1894] AC 57.

[9] Williams (1987) 84 CrAppR 299; c.f. Fulcher [1995] 2 CrAppR 251.

[10] Pettmann (1985) (unreported), quote with approval in Fulcher (previous note).

[11] Wright 90 CrAppR 325. The case decides that, on a charge of sexual offences against children, evidence is not admissible to show that the defendant, when charged with buggery on youths, had a propensity to commit buggery with males. The same would apply, a fortiori, to evidence showing a tendency to abuse them violently.

[12] [2000] 2 AC 483.

[13] Originally S.1(f) (ii), and renumbered by the Youth Justice and Criminal Evidence Act 1999.

[14] E.g. Marsh [1994] Criminal Law Review 52, where under this provision a defendant prosecuted for an assault committed on the rugby field was cross-examined about his

disciplinary record for violent play.

[15] Criminal Evidence Act 1989 S.1 (3) (iii) (formerly S.1 (f) (iii)).

[16] Lowery v R [1974] AC 85; Bracewell (1978) 68 CrAppR 44.

[17] Indictment Rules 1971, Rule 9.

[18] Ludlow v Metropolitan Police Commissioner [1971] AC 29.

[19] R v H [1995] AC 596.

[20] Glanville Williams, *The Proof of Guilt,* (3rd ed. 1963) p.214.

[21] Justice for All, Cm 5563 (July 2002), p.80.

[22] "Scene" is referred to in this protocol as the child's home. This is assuming that the child died at home and is still there when the police and other professionals attend. However, on many occasions the child will already have been taken to the hospital. If this is the case, the principles remain the same. However, in such a situation, there may be two scenes and resources will need to be allocated accordingly. It is important to note that if the child has already been moved from the home, this does not negate the need for professionals to visit the home.